Acquiring Time

Book 2 – Beyond Success Series

by

Mary Čolak

Published in 2022 by Discourse Books, Victoria, BC, Canada

www.marycolak.com

Cover design by impact studios

Library and Archives Canada Cataloguing in Publication
Acquiring time: Beyond success / Mary Čolak

Includes bibliographical footnotes.
Paperback: ISBN 978-1-7778086-1-7
Electronic book: ISBN 978-1-7778086-3-1

1. Business & Economics / Time Management
2. Business & Economics / Personal Success
3. Self-help / Personal Growth / Success

****

We can never find more time. We can only create it.

****

Dedication

For Nikola, with whom I spend most of my time.

Coming Soon

Beyond Success Series

Lean Productivity and Efficiency
Communicating for Results
Getting a Handle on Records

Book 1 in this series:
Considerations in Making Money

Acquiring Time
Book 2 Beyond Success Series
Contents

Introduction

What does time mean to you? Is it robbing, killing, or controlling you? Is it saving you? Or are you the master of your time?

Regardless of your response to these questions, whether we acknowledge time as a precious commodity is irrelevant because time is a gift, bar none. The fantastic thing about time is that no one is so powerful that they can make it stop or slow down. Therefore, time is endless because we cannot determine its beginning or end. However, our human existence makes time finite—a limited resource within a fixed period—and, therefore, valuable.

Consider that we live in a realm of existence that includes length, width, height, and depth. Overarching these dimensions is time, an abstract measure that is infinite and limited. According to the general theory of relativity, space (i.e., the universe) emerged in the Big Bang about 14 billion years ago. Before that, an extremely tiny dot comprised all matter. That dot also contained the matter that later came to be the sun, the Earth, and the moon – the heavenly bodies that tell us about the passing of time. Before the Big Bang, there was no space or time; however, that is just a theory.

A curious element about space is that it represents time through change, such as the circular motion of the moon around the Earth. Likewise, we see time change and circular motion in the four seasons with the Earth revolving around the sun. Thus, the passing of time undeniably connects to the concept of space. In addition, time continually moves forward, never backward (unless someone discovers a way to experience time travel into the past – I suppose anything is possible).

Grounded in today's reality, our understanding of time is that it spreads across 365.25 days in a year in 12 months ranging from 28 to 31 days per month, 24 hours per day, 60 minutes per hour, 60 seconds per minute, and so on to the tiniest time measurement. We schedule appointments and meetings based on a particular hour and minute on a specific day within a certain month and year. We do all this almost absentmindedly, never considering the fundamental nature of time.

Subsequently, although we are aware of the passing of time, we cannot, with certainty, say what exactly happens when time passes. However, our life and time are inseparable – every thought and feeling we have and every action we undertake uses time.

Perhaps one of the most peculiar qualities of time is that we use motion to measure the passing of time. Thus, time is evident by movement. For example, old-style clocks tick away the seconds using motion—I can see and hear my office clock ticking each second as its arm moves from right to left around the clock's face, without fail. Still, the curious thing about this ticking sound is that I cannot hear it when I am focused on writing, but that does not mean that time is standing still.

Understanding that we cannot stop time, our only option to get the most value from our time is to control how we use it. Therefore, controlling our time is within our power, and becoming a wise time manager is within our reach. How we use our time determines our standard and quality of life. When we master our time, we get more done, become energized, and get to do more of the things we enjoy—we don't hear the clock ticking away the seconds.

While time may be the biggest riddle of our universe, it does not have to be a riddle in your life. You can use your time effectively to make the best decisions and take the best actions to live your best life at home and work. Notwithstanding, one of the critical considerations in time management is value. How much value do you contribute each hour of your day at work and, for that matter, at home? For example, do chats with coworkers about last night's sporting event add value to your work? Do endless company meetings without clear action items add value to the company (or you)? How much utility do you contribute each hour that you spend at home? How much quality time do you spend with your children or other family members and friends? Or is your quality time spent online debating with strangers?

Despite being a hot topic for decades, time management remains an uncontested focus on personal skills without considering why problems arise and why these problems are common. We still need research to investigate how the work context and time use exert pressure on task content and social influences. For example, does a person have the autonomy to self-manage their activities, including delegation and rejection of work requests? Several factors can and do impact our ability to manage our time. However, these human-caused factors are usually within our control.

This collection of my favourite posts provides unique insights into time management (and time-wasting) that I hope will help you turn your time into an ally and inspire you to use your time wisely. After all, time truly is a precious resource for each of us.

Keeping Time

Since Earth's beginning, humans have measured time in various ways by observing nature, especially the four seasons. But it's not just nature that helped us track time. More than 30,000 years ago, people carved notches into mammoth tusks to follow the moon and stars. For example, Stonehenge is one of the oldest monolithic structures for marking time and ceremonies. In addition, people used another structure, the 4,100-year-old Chinese observatory at Shanxi, for sacrificial rites and astronomical observations. Regions also tracked time through weather events like summer flooding in the Nile that signaled another completed year. From monolithic structures to slivers of matter, people have kept precise time.

These and other experiences with time-tracking have led to increasing precision over millennia, from sundials dividing days into hours and clocks dividing hours into quarters, minutes, and seconds. As our timepieces evolved, so did our zeal for ever-more exact timekeeping. For instance, we went from sundials to water clocks,[1] mechanical clocks, electric clocks, and atomic clocks. In addition, scientists developed devices that relied on microscopic nuclear movements.[2] For example, the second, our smallest temporal unit, is critical to our modern timekeeping systems embedded in geographical positioning systems (GPS) and cellphones. Did you know that today's atomic clocks are so accurate that they won't lose a second over 15 billion years?

While many of us take our global system of timekeeping mainly for granted, consider that we have 24 time zones stemming outward from Greenwich.[3] These time zones include a year equivalent to 12 months, divided into 52 weeks, and recognized from San

Francisco to Shanghai, including the much-debated biannual daylight saving time. These standards allow us to manage our daily lives without complication and on schedule.

But when did we get so obsessed with time and time management?

It turns out that this is not a modern phenomenon. It started sometime in ancient Egypt around 1771 B.C. with Hammurabi's Code. Hammurabi was Babylon's ruler, and he developed the code to regulate Mesopotamian society. The code's impact on time is that it established a minimum wage for workers, calculating wages in days, months, years, and even per project/task. The code also based compensation on professions. For example, doctors got paid more than field workers.[4] Here are a few curious payment stipulations from Hammurabi's Code:

#48. If anyone owes a debt for a loan, and a storm prostrates the grain, or the harvest fails, or the grain does not grow for lack of water; in that year, he need not give his creditor any grain; he washes his debt tablet in water and pays no rent for this year.

#221. If a physician heals a man's broken bone or diseased soft part, the patient shall pay the physician five shekels in money.[5]

#224. If a veterinary surgeon performs a serious operation on an ass or an ox and cures it, the owner shall pay the surgeon one-sixth of a shekel.

In addition, since the ancient Egyptian economy relied on the distribution of goods, workers received wages in meals.[6] But how did the employers track workers' time? It appears that clay tablets[7] invented around 3100–3000 BC in Mesopotamia (southern Iraq) were the payroll books of the ancients. Employers recorded workers' daily wages in cuneiform (meaning: "wedge-shaped") writing,[8] including symbols for bread, grain, radishes, beer, and other food products. Most experts believe that the earliest writing was in the Sumerian language (now extinct), which emerged in southern Iraq around 3200 BC. Early writing is also interesting due to its value in accounting for time, but not literature, letters, or other present-day practices.

Time tracking became even more necessary as we evolved from ancient times and entered the Industrial Revolution in Britain in the 18th century. Benjamin Franklin's famous aphorism, "Time is money,"[9] is perhaps the best description of the relationship between employees and employers then—and I dare say it still holds substantial meaning today.

Fast-forward to 1888: Willard Le Grand Bundy, a jeweler from New York, invents the time clock. Here we now have our first machine to record hours worked. Many manufacturing companies used similar devices to manage attendance and calculate employee hours following this invention. However, Frederick Winslow Taylor,[10] considered the "father of scientific management," was the first to launch today's time management foundation.

His time management started as a quest to increase productivity in manufacturing, focusing on the efficiency of individual workers, and quickly spread to the office and home. Taylor looked for the one best way to do every job. In addition to Taylor, the husband-and-wife team of Frank and Lillian Gilbreth also impacted work by introducing time and motion studies in the manufacturing process.

Moreover, some professions turned to paper timesheets, away from time stamp machines. For example, consulting and legal firms needed to keep track of hours for client billing. Thus, in 1943, Reginald Heber Smith, a lawyer, introduced the paper timesheet as a cost accounting tool. But it wasn't until the 1950s that the American Bar Association promoted billable hours for lawyers to increase their income. The Association issued a pamphlet titled "The 1958 Lawyer and His 1938 Dollar" to promulgate the idea of billable hours to replace fixed fees. Thus, in its simplest form, timekeeping became popular in the 1950s and 1960s.

Time management, the flip side of timekeeping, is a tool intended to help individuals make better use of available time—it stipulates "do's" and "don't's"—and guides individuals to focus on efficiency and productivity. In other words, if you spend two hours of your day checking social media posts, those are two hours that, if allocated elsewhere, could enhance your time. For instance, you could spend those two hours preparing dinner, engaging with your family, following up with your co-worker, or writing that report you've been putting off for the past week.

Time management also focuses on solving problems. For example, if you are feeling overwhelmed with your workload, this could indicate poor time management. Another example is procrastination. Therefore, planning and preparation are the way to prevent these and other issues. In addition, good time management practices can lead to improved outcomes such as increased performance and less tension. However, research lacks studies on time management models. For instance, one study found a beneficial relationship between perceived control of time and stress; however, research on job performance is scant.[11]

Today, timekeeping machines and paper timesheets have given way to biometric data, radio frequency identification (RFID) tags, and other technologies that automate data processing and prevent time frauds like the buddy clock-in system.[12] Automated timekeeping avoids calculation errors and includes functionality to help company owners determine vital business data. However, no matter the timekeeping accuracy, just because someone "clocks" in for work does not guarantee productive work.

While wrought with good intentions, timekeeping has a dark side—our quest for efficiency led to worker alienation. It wasn't until interventions from human resource groups that working relationships started improving. Businesses went from remote offices to cubicles without doors, including landscaped offices and, in some cases, Christmas bonuses. In addition, organizations eliminated time clocks and introduced regular meetings to improve communication. Regardless of the physical improvements, businesses still had one aim: to maximize employee productivity and ensure time spent at work was quality time.

Today's digital era is once again dehumanizing our work environment. Smartphones and computers are exceptional at scheduling time and alerting us to meetings and appointments. Still, they are also decreasing our in-person interactions, reducing our creativity, and somehow putting us back into Taylor's scientific management era. The curious thing is that we are doing this willingly. With all this technology, our need for time management is more extensive than ever because as technology increases our pace of life, our need for time management also significantly increases.

How smartphone apps, virtual-reality headsets, and Big Data will change our lives remains to be seen. Consequently, technology can make our lives better or worse—we have that choice. Technology enables time, and how we use our time shapes our shared future. If anything, the global history of time reform should remind us that technology makes no promises. What we ask technology to do for us will make all the difference in our lives but know this: technology can give us more or less time depending on our choices. Timekeeping helps us lead more productive lives, including effectiveness and life balance, but the secret is in how we manage our time.

Timekeeping and time management rest in our individual differences and how well we can plan and attend to our time. However, this does not mean that your time management capabilities are genetic—they most certainly are not. Everyone is capable of applying good time management concepts. Our differences depend on time urgency (the degree to which our focus is on time), polychronicity (our preference for multitasking), and time use efficiency. Ultimately, our choices will determine how we keep our time.

Time and Goals

Do you know where you spend your time when you are at work? You might say, of course you know. You spend your time working. Silly question. But seriously, what is the point of your activities at work (or at home, for that matter)? Do you know your goal(s) relating to your activities? Let me explain.

Consider that time is valuable—if for no other reason than it is finite for each of us, albeit infinite at the same time. That said, where we spend our time must matter to us. If we value our time, we will ensure that what we do with our time is carefully allocated to the things that matter, whether at work or home. This allocation of time is where goals become essential.

When you are at work, what is your goal? Are you there to watch the clock tick away eight hours and then go home? Are you there to make a difference in the organization's bottom line? Are you there to learn and create and grow intellectually? Whatever your goal, know that a time element is associated with building your success.

How do you create success through wise use of time? Goals.

You create your goals by choosing how you spend your time, including the steps you need to follow to realize your goals. Thus, accomplishing your goals means determining how you will invest your time. However, don't get me wrong. Goals are not only about work and business. Goals also include personal objectives. For example, how much time do you wish to spend at work versus at home? What is a good ratio for you? Or how much money is enough for you? And what standard of health do you wish to attain?

There are goals, and then there are effective goals. It is easy to say, "I want to own an island one day," but how realistic or effective is that goal? Effective goals must be realistic; the best goals are those set by the person affected. It makes no sense for me to say, "John, your goal for today/this week/month/year is to re-build the Tesla Model 3 electrical system." Why? Because John may not be interested in electrical systems, he may not have the requisite expertise or other reasons. John must set his goals to have a good chance of accomplishing them.

To set effective goals, here are five considerations.

1. Achievable. Goals must be realistic (as described above: see the "island ownership" goal example). If you aim for an impossible accomplishment, it will remain impossible. However, even if a goal appears to be impossible initially, if you break out the goal into smaller achievable pieces, there is a chance that maybe you can achieve the impossible. If you are excited about accomplishing the impossible, give it a go. Don't let others discourage you. For example, I dreamed that I would write a book one day. So I did a lot of research into how to get the project done, including writing the steps to get me there. I achieved my goal.

2. Stretch. Goals must make you "stretch" a bit to achieve them. If your plan does not challenge you in some way—physically, mentally, socially—then there's a good chance you will not find the motivation to reach the goal. So instead, make the goal demanding enough to give you purpose and go for that goal. For example, my goal of writing a book was demanding; it made me

stretch out of my comfort zone, but I persisted until I reached my goal.

3. SMART. The "SMART" principle in setting goals and objectives is specific, measurable, attainable, realistic, and timely. Make sure your goals meet all five criteria. Remember, if you can't measure it, you can't attain it. For example, my SMART goal was: specific (write a book), measurable (I will write at least one chapter per week), attainable (I have the book material, computer, and computer software necessary to write my book), realistic (my book covers business topics with which I am very familiar), and timely (I will write my book by 2022).

4. Flexible. Be sure you build flexibility into attaining your goals. For example, if you want to own an island in ten years but a world crisis derails your plans, build in that cushion to extend your timeline. It's always good to have risk management planning with any goal. Without flexibility, we become demotivated to achieve our goals. In my book writing, I allowed flexibility by making my deadline 2022, not specifically a month or day in 2022.

5. Written. If you carry your goals in your head, there's a high likelihood that you will forget them and, consequently, never reach them. On the other hand, if you are serious about your goals, then write them – it could be on paper or electronically. The key is writing your goals and reviewing your progress regularly. "Out of sight, out of mind" should not be your goal motto. For example, when I planned to write my book, I created a Word file of a draft book outline. I also made a new

folder to store all my research material relating to the book topic.

How you manage your time will make the difference in how and whether you achieve your goals. That's it. Simple.

Apply the above elements of effective goal-making to three areas of your life: personal, organizational, and career. In personal goals, think about how your overall success looks and feels. What do you want to accomplish in your life? Do you want to get married? Have children? A big/small house? Five cars? Manage/ own a Fortune 500 company? Shake the world up with new ideas? What?

In your organizational goals, consider what contributions you wish to make to your organization. For example, do you desire to make new friends/colleagues /mentors while at work? Do you want to modify the organization's purchasing processes to help the organization become more successful? Do you wish to learn from superiors to become an executive leader eventually?

Finally, what do you want to achieve in the next week/month/year/two or more years in your career? How will you achieve your goals? Write your goals to track your success. Don't forget the SMART principles.

Here's to using your time effectively to achieve everything you desire.

REFLECTION

- What is your personal goal? What does personal success look like for you?
- What is your organizational goal? Do you want to achieve a sustainable relationship between you and your organization?
- Consider how your success may hinge on your organization's success. For example, if you improve the organization's purchasing system, would that bring you closer to a management role?
- What do you want to achieve next week?
- What do you want to achieve next month?
- What do you want to achieve this year?
- What would you do with an extra hour per day? Think of two personal things and two professional things. Then, to motivate yourself to pursue those things in that extra hour per day, answer the question: "What's in it for me to achieve these goals?"

How Much is Your Time Worth?

In my book, *Considerations for Making Money*, I discuss how inefficient organizations and people waste time, which inevitably translates to considerable losses. The curious thing about wasted time is most people don't stop to think about the value of their wasted time.

Whether you work for an organization or yourself, you offer your time in return for money. Therefore, saved money is saved time, gained money is gained time, and lost money is lost/wasted time. For instance, if you make $100 per hour and spend three hours per day in meetings that add no benefit to your job, you just wasted $300 of your (or your organization's) money. However, not everybody's time has the same market value. Therefore, the bigger your performance, the more you get per time unit.

Here's an interesting twist when it comes to time and money. Saving money short-term can waste time long-term. In other words, when we consider our time, we also need to consider quality—bad quality is expensive, whether it is a poorly written report or an inexpensive chair.

For example, if you paid a fraction of the price to a consultant to write a recommendations report for your department, but the recommendations are impractical, you just bought yourself a lousy quality product. The same goes for an inexpensive chair that will break in a couple of years versus purchasing an original Eames chair that will last a lifetime. In both cases, you lost money buying poor quality. You wasted money and, as a result, you wasted your time.

Attention and care can save time. Therefore, it is worth investing your time into planning (i.e., decision-making) before spending your time (or money) on products or services. This investment is also indisputable for the quality time you spend with people you care about, whether at home or work.

Ultimately, while we can count time and money, not everything boils down to money. For instance, do you measure your life in dollars spent or saved? Probably not. You measure your life in years spent well. Therefore, your most valuable resource is your time.

Next time you think about working overtime or picking up an extra shift, recall your purpose for spending your time this way. Time is precious. Do not waste it on things that add no value to you or your employer.

REFLECTION

- Where does your time go? Keep a journal for one week to track your time to understand where you spend quality time and where you waste time. Now add up your wasted time and multiply it by your hourly rate. Is that number a shock to you?
- What will you do to stop wasting time?
- How will you determine your quality work and spend more time doing it?

Capitalizing on Strengths

Do you feel "stuck" in a job? And before the end of the workday, can you hardly wait to get out of the office? If so, you may be in the wrong job.

Feeling stuck may signal that you are not using your strengths in your current job. As a result, if you aren't using your talents, resentment builds, and frustration ensues. Not only that, you are not productive on the job – think "deadwood," and you'll get the idea. Let me explain.

Let's say you're a decision-maker by nature but find yourself in a job where you neither contribute nor make organization-wide decisions. As a result, you second-guess the organization's decisions. Then you start resenting its decision-makers. In addition, you start disliking your boss and co-workers because you see them as part of the problem.

You might say that you can't help it; you need to work somewhere. Fair enough. At some point in our careers, most of us end up in temporary jobs that are nothing more than a way to pay the bills. But for long-term career happiness and productivity, you need to understand your strengths to best use your time at work and home.

In addition to identifying strengths, we must understand how we work best and how we work best depends on our personalities. Our personality determines how we perform, no matter what we do—from organizing our breakfast in the morning to processing our daily tasks and relating to people. Each of us has an inherent capability of how we manage our "to-do's."

Consider this fact: While it is possible to modify our habits, few (if any) people can outright change their strengths or habits. Instead, we can *identify* our strengths and habits and then choose to improve both in a way that moves us further in our careers. Thus, to catapult your career to the next level, I compiled five ways to help you improve your strengths.

1. Pay attention to feedback. What do others say about your strengths? What do they notice about you? Sometimes, we instinctively know what we're good at but become blind to our capabilities for whatever reason. It may take several people to point out your talents before you start to pay attention.

2. Tune in to your performance. How do you produce your best work? Is it by working alone or in teams? Do you prefer to learn through reading, listening, or viewing? What time of day are you most productive, and why at that time? By understanding "how" you work, you will appreciate the unique characteristics of what comprises an ideal workday for you and when you are most productive (cue: effective time management).

3. Notice what gives you energy. When working on a task, does it make you feel tired, bored, overwhelmed, interested, or challenged? Does the task motivate you to work even harder to get the job done? Do you feel alive? If the work makes you feel energized (even if you're physically tired), then that's the type of work you need to do—you have found your passion, your niche.

4. Do not compromise your values. The place where you work must reflect your values. The organization's policies should align with its practices. In other words, the organization should practice what it preaches. If your

beliefs align with the organization's culture, you have a match made in heaven.

5. Contribute like there's no tomorrow. Endeavour to improve the organization's systems, processes, methods, policies, and other practices based on your strengths. Your contribution will positively impact the organization and help you feel a sense of accomplishment. You know your strengths serve you well if you feel you have accomplished something.

Roman philosopher Lucius Annaeus Seneca said, *"Luck is what happens when preparation meets opportunity."* Substitute "career" for the word "luck," and you can see how using your strengths can help you build a happy and productive career where you don't waste your time. Now substitute "life" for "luck"—the sky's the limit if you are willing to reach for it.

REFLECTION

- How do you use your strengths in your job?
- How do you use your strengths at home?
- What is your proudest work achievement?
- What is your proudest non-work achievement?
- How did your strengths contribute to your achievement?
- What can you do to recognize your strengths more often at work and home?

Best Time Efficiency Hacks for the Generations

How one saves time depends on who you speak to and their age. Each generation has an affinity for different efficiency tools and techniques. For example, Baby Boomers (born between 1946 and 1964) tend to opt for multitasking because they believe that doing more than one thing at a time saves time (guilty as charged!). The truth is it doesn't. Multitasking is counterproductive and decreases efficiency. Perhaps Boomers' nonconformist ways make them stick to their beliefs. Boomers' labels of themselves range from self-obsessed to stuck in their ways. Boomers are unlikely to change their habits at this stage—unless they can buy it and it's easy to assemble. This fact must surely remind one of the saying, "you can't teach an old dog new tricks."

Gen Xers (born between 1965 and 1976) are often labeled the "slacker" generation. They appear to be uncommitted, unfocused, and disorganized. In addition, they tend to move between jobs frequently, preferring a balanced lifestyle over the financial comfort their parents craved. But like with all labels, it's not usually a "one size fits all" (e.g., not all Baby Boomers are multitaskers). So if you're a GenXer looking to improve your efficiency, here is what you can do:

- Close all applications on your computer besides the one on which you are currently working. This action will help you maintain focus.
- Work in small manageable chunks rather than tackling the whole project at once.

Working like this will help you reduce overwhelm.

- When something needs doing, do it right away. If you think about it for too long, you may procrastinate and not get the job done correctly (or on time).
- If a task is tedious or frustrating, think of something else that you might be doing that may be worse. Then use that comparison to start working on the task at hand.
- Every hour, take a ten-minute break to refresh. As a result, you will have more energy and focus on attending to the task.

Generation Y, also called "Millennials" (born between 1977 and 1994), is the largest cohort since the Baby Boomers. They are labeled as lazy, debt-ridden, and programmed for instant gratification. Some employers portray them as demanding and unrealistic in their career aspirations. They also tend to be Internet-addicted and lonely.

Millennials don't mind working hard, but they want others to judge them on their output and results rather than the total hours they spend on the task. So their time efficiency hack is leveraging technology to help them gain greater work-life balance. In other words, they will automate anything to save time. If you're a millennial, here are some efficiency hacks for millennials by millennials:

- When not in a mental state to work, hit the gym or run. Don't forget to shower before returning to work.
- Return phone calls while waiting for the bus, taxi, airplane, or ferry.
- When you have an idea, chase it until you figure it out. If you don't, the idea may drive you nuts and lead you to procrastinate and be overwhelmed.

- Instead of a computer, use an e-reader for reading books – the lack of multitasking helps you maintain focus because you cannot switch between windows with a browser.
- Make friends that can save you time – for instance, if your friends love to browse online for the best deals, get them to tell you when they find a great deal. Then, all you have to do is "click" to buy; you don't need to do the homework.
- Allocate one hour daily to handle email and other "to-do's" that you need to clear off your list. This activity can be at the beginning or end of the day but is a must for saving time.

Generation Z, the iPad generation (born between 1995 and 2012), grew up with the Internet. They are incredibly technology-savvy. You can bet that whatever efficiency hack they use will involve technology in the workforce.

Generation Alpha (born from 2010 onward) will likely be the most formally educated generation in history. They began school earlier (think pre-school or daycare at two or three years of age) and will study longer. Moreover, these children are from older, wealthier parents with fewer siblings, and some are already labeling them as materialistic (Baby Boomers, déjà vu?).

Regardless of which generation defines you, the best way to be efficient is to rest when you need to, get over your overwhelm, don't procrastinate, plan your days, and use your "to-do" lists to monitor your progress toward your goals.

REFLECTION

- Which of the above generations defines your habits?
- How can you turn your generational habit(s) into a time efficiency hack?
- How can you make time work for you?
- What advice would you give the generation that came before you regarding time management?
- What advice would you give the generation that comes after you regarding time management?

Improving Productivity by Working from Home

Does working from home improve productivity? A Stanford University study[13] of a Chinese travel agency concluded that it does. The study found that employees working from home:

- Were 13% more productive (9% worked more hours, took fewer breaks and sick days, and 4% had higher performance rates per minute – hypothesized to be due to quieter working conditions).
- Had 50% less attrition.
- Reported higher feelings of work satisfaction.
- Increased total factor productivity between 20–30% (the increase was due to two sources – efficiency in calls per minute and capital input). In addition, the company estimated annual savings of $1,900 per employee.

The learning from the experiment includes the following:

- Working from home improves performance.
- Allowing employees a choice generated a far more significant effect than requiring employees to work from home or the office.
- Management was surprised by the dramatic drop in attrition.

In addition to benefits to employees and employers due to working from home, society sees benefits. These benefits include choosing where one wishes to live (instead of close to the employer's office), less pollution and traffic congestion from work commutes, and better family and community life because of the flexible hours.

However, improving productivity and saving money by having employees work from home does not work (pardon the pun) for everyone. People need to recognize whether they have the discipline to perform as well as, or better than, working in an office environment. Also, some individuals need the socializing that comes with working in an office – these individuals cannot thrive in isolation. Others must strike a careful balance.

Self-control and pride in one's work are mandatory for working from home. Completing tasks and communicating effectively with others is also a requirement. Trust is another considerable element when working from home – employers need to trust that their employees are doing their best, but they also need to respect schedules and expectations.

I work from home most of the time, and I cannot be happier about this arrangement. My most rewarding client work occurs when I am in my home office. This feeling of reward is likely because I am disciplined and have the necessary self-control about my work. It also helps that I love what I do.

As a supplement to this article, the pandemic forced many people to work from home. A U.S. survey in October 2020 of 10,332 adults found that the majority (64%) currently work from home because their businesses are closed. However, 60% of respondents indicated that they prefer working from home. In addition, about seven in ten workers stated that they are teleworking all or most of the time. This finding and similar surveys indicate that there may be a new trend favoring telework.[14]

REFLECTION

- Would you work from home if your job is conducive to working from home? Explain.
- What changes would you need to make at home to accommodate your ability to work from home? Are these changes feasible?
- Do you foresee more people working from home soon? Explain.
- What is the driving factor(s) for working from home? Is it your driving factor? Explain.

Drugs and Workplace Productivity

Productivity doesn't just happen. It takes focus and sustained effort to accomplish work tasks. However, the amount of focus and effort varies depending on the task's difficulty. The opposite is also true. That is, non-productivity is so easy – that's why many of us can slide into a weekend of relaxation without any effort.

But while at work, we must do our best to be as productive as possible. And to do that, it is equally important to respect our bodies and not use substances that can inhibit our work performance. Ever. According to the National Council on Alcoholism and Drug Dependence, drug abuse costs employers $81 billion annually.[15] It also affects one out of every five families.

In addition, workers who report having three or more jobs in the previous five years are about twice as likely to be current or past-year users of illegal drugs than those with two or fewer jobs. An astounding 70% of the estimated 14.8 million employed Americans use illicit drugs. The Canadian Centre on Substance Abuse in 2013 estimated that legal substances (tobacco and alcohol) accounted for 79.3% of the total cost of substance abuse, while illegal drugs accounted for 20.7% ($8.2 billion) of costs.

However, data for 2017 suggests that costs from tobacco and alcohol are around $13 billion, followed by opioids at $4.25 billion, combined central nervous system (CNS) stimulants and depressants are $1.5 billion, cocaine at $983 million, and cannabis at $550 million. Therefore, despite the year range from 2003 to 2017, tobacco and alcohol still account for the most significant use of legal substance costs. Moreover, these numbers can only increase with the recent explosion of "medical marijuana" retailers. As a result, employers now find themselves in a situation where they need to consider the impacts of once-illicit drugs on their workforce.

The impacts on work productivity and time management are hard to ignore. With more countries legalizing cannabis, one should not overlook this drug's immediate and ongoing effect on productivity in the workplace, not to mention potentially detrimental health effects. Documented evidence shows that cannabis causes the following side effects (this is not a complete list):[16]

- Decreased focus
- Decreased concentration
- Decreased alertness
- Decreased memory and thinking capabilities
- Decreased motivation impacting the employee's ability to relate to their colleagues, clients, and customers
- Increased risk of developing dependence
- Increased risk of respiratory illness
- Increased risk of mental illness
- Diminished relationships – think about how this impacts teamwork in the workplace with added pressure on non-users, including poor collaboration and concentration on projects (as an example)
- Increased absenteeism
- Increased risk of injury of self or others (resulting in loss of time and potential workers' compensation)
- Decreased driving performance

In 2012, marijuana was Canada's most commonly used illicit drug, with 10.6% of Canadians reporting past-year use. In addition, Canadian youth had the highest rate of past-year marijuana use (28% in 2009–2010) compared to students in other developed countries. This number increased in 2018–2019 to 32.4%.[17]

Canada legalized cannabis in October 2018. A survey in 2020 of marijuana usage in Canada showed the following: in 2017, 15% of Canadians age 15 and older (or 4.4 million) have used cannabis in the past 12 months (19% among those 15 to 19 years; 33% among the 20 to 24 age group; and 13% among age 25 years and older). In 2018/19, a Canadian survey indicates that 18% of students in grades 7 to 12 (approximately 374,000) have used cannabis in the past 12 months.[18]

While governments are starting to "give in" to the demand for legalizing marijuana, this legalization has put the onus on organizations to conduct workplace drug testing. In addition, organizations need to ensure adequate workforce training in identifying potential drug use. As a result, human resource departments are even more critical to the organizations' functions to ensure that drug use does not impact the business's bottom line.

How HR can help is by building relationships with managers and employees. When you know someone, it's much easier to identify changes in behavior and productivity and provide proper intervention. In addition, implementing policies and procedures will help all workers be aware of the signs and symptoms of drug use. Much like personal issues or inter-staff and management issues, keeping substance use/abuse top of mind helps identify the problem to address it quickly.

REFLECTION

- What do you do to maintain your optimal health?
- What else can you do to maintain your optimal health and enjoy your time to the fullest?
- Have you witnessed drug or alcohol impairment at work? What did you notice about the person's work performance?
- What would you do if you knew a co-worker was alcohol or drug-impaired at work? Why?

Improving Work Performance

How's your productivity? Does the mere mention of the word stir unease? And what about all those uber-organized work colleagues? How are they on top of their work, yet you feel a constant struggle to keep up?

You may be surprised to learn there's no secret to improving work performance. It's all about being organized. And the best part of all is that it's a skill anyone can learn. Improving work performance is about being productive. It's about doing the right things in the right way to yield maximum output. It's about planning and prioritizing to make that happen. And it's also about protecting your time. So, let's cut to the chase – here are ten suggestions to help you be more productive and use your time efficiently.

1. Arrange your physical work environment. Organize your workspace so that everything you use has a "home." Then, after use, always return items to their home. This practice takes discipline and a lot of work initially but becomes a habit with practice.

2. Arrange your electronic files. Electronic files arranged in a hierarchy enable cross-organizational sharing, resulting in less duplication of files, no silos of information, and dramatically improved retrieval time. In addition, use a functional subject-based classification system for optimum efficiency and productivity (e.g., libraries use a similar system).

3. Use appropriate tools. No amount of arranging or organizing will help you work at your best if your devices are out-of-date. Are you still using Windows 95? Or DOS (do you even remember DOS)? Invest in current technology, a friendlier website, and appropriate resources to help you be more productive. Not investing will bog you down, create frustration, and lead to regularly "burning the midnight oil."

4. Check in with your list. As you make commitments, write them on a paper calendar or schedule them in your email calendar, and check in with your list daily. Lists help us manage our time and free our minds of mental energy that we would otherwise spend on tracking our "to-do's." If you write what you need to do instead of keeping it in your head, you'll also experience less stress and better sleep. I keep my lists in my email calendar because email is one of those certain business functions I check daily.

5. Do it now. If a task takes five minutes or less—at work or home—then do it now. If it will take longer, write it on your list and schedule time to do the task. Organized people don't procrastinate on completing tasks that take only a few minutes.

6. Uni-task. While multitasking may seem like you're accomplishing more, you accomplish less across more areas. To be truly efficient, effective, and productive, focus on one task, giving it your full attention. Turn off email pop-ups and calendar reminders. Protect your time to gain fruitful results.

7. Problem-solve; don't blame. Use a problem-solving approach if you get sidetracked or encounter a challenge that impacts your work. One of the things I notice about proactive people is that when they have a complaint, they always accompany the complaint with a possible solution. For example, if you feel you just spent a lot of time attending classes, but can't seem to grasp the course concepts, perhaps the solution is to spend more time learning the ideas instead of rushing through the material.

8. Work with your energy cycle. Work to suit your daily energy levels instead of time management for the sake of time management. For example, if you have high energy in the morning, that is the time to do your most difficult or creative work. Conversely, don't work on critical tasks when your energy is at a lull.

9. Know thyself. Organized people know their strengths and weaknesses and reflect a high sense of self-worth. So ask for help to complete work on time. Just because it's in your job description does not mean you need to do it all yourself. Instead, think of your time as a resource that has value. Perfectionists and high achievers may not be comfortable letting anyone else share the reins, but interpersonal support goes a long way in managing stress.

10. De-stress. Most people operate from chronic stress, but those who can focus and stay organized can manage stress. The most effective way to manage stress is to exercise every day for at least 30 minutes. Exercise

can include a brisk walk, meditation, yoga, or whatever works for you – just don't sit at your computer all day. Full disclosure: sometimes I spend seemingly endless hours at my computer without a break, but I try to make that a rare "habit."

Practicing the above suggestions takes motivation to get started. However, the habit will keep you moving to become more organized and productive once started. As a result, you will also experience more "free" time and become a happier person.

REFLECTION

- Of the above suggestions, which one do you need to work on most (i.e., priority)?
- How will you tackle this priority?
- Remember to build a support network for those days that you may falter on improving your number one priority. The support network could be as easy as setting a reminder in your pop-up email calendar to remind you to do what you said you would do. Alternatively, having a friend check in with you daily via email or text is also an option.

Where Does Time Go?

Do you know where you spend most of your time? Like many of us, you probably think you know where you spend your time, but surprisingly, there's a good chance that you don't. Think about your days at work or home; wherever you spend most days is an appropriate example. Now consider those days when nothing seems to go right or the time just flies by or never ends. You likely remember the slow, dull days but not the great days.

To understand where we spend most of our time and where we should be spending most of our time, what I find helpful is keeping a time log for about a week; sometimes, even a month is good to get a feel for those extraordinary time spends. Tracking your time in a time log helps you see where you spend your time and highlights your habits. However, changing habits is a story for another post.

The great thing about time logs is that they provide the research necessary to identify what percentage of your time you spend on important, urgent, routine, and non-essential tasks (i.e., a useless task adds no value to you or your organization).

Use a spreadsheet or even a piece of paper to track your time. Here is an example of the columns to maintain for the period of your log (e.g., seven to 30 days). Put the date at the top of each sheet of the log. Here are the column headings.

Time	Task	Minutes Used	Priority	Comment
This column is the start time of the task (e.g., 8:00 a.m.)	Write the task in this column (e.g., meeting with Joe, I called Helen, staff meeting, lunch, writing a project proposal, etc.).	This column is the number of minutes you took for the specific task (e.g., 10, 15, etc.). You could also track your time in hours (e.g., .25 hours, 1.5 hours, etc.), whatever is appropriate for you.	1 = urgent (i.e., think life or death) 2 = important (i.e., must get done, is valuable to the organization or me) 3 = routine (i.e., needs doing but can wait) 4 = not essential (i.e., if you don't do it, no one would likely notice very soon)	This column is for anything specific that stands out about the task (e.g., sidetracked by an urgent work better during the task).

When you know where you spend your time, you can identify where you need more time and what areas you should reduce (i.e., timewasters). For example, most people spend their work time on phone calls, visitors, looking for information (online or in the records room), meeting with clients, meeting with staff and others (e.g., coworkers), unplanned meetings, paperwork, or crises.

Reviewing your log, do you notice anything that distracted you from your work priorities? What could you have done (or do) to avoid these distractions in the future? What tasks took longer than you would have liked? Take note of all these and other items that you could potentially reduce next time they occur.

By getting a handle on where we spend our time, we are in an excellent position to allocate our time to areas of value that lead to improved conditions for success in our personal, organizational, and career initiatives.

REFLECTION

- Reviewing your time log, what was your most prolonged period of uninterrupted time?
- What things did you do that you could have delegated?
- How many interruptions did you record?
- Which communications took too long?
- How much time did you spend in meetings? Were the meetings productive?
- How much time did you spend waiting on others?
- How much time did you spend re-doing work (e.g., re-working documents)?
- Of your tasks each day, what was the number one timewaster for you? How can you handle this differently next time?
- Of your tasks each day, what was the task that added the most value to your day? How can you do more of these tasks in the future?

Bouncing Around

Did you know that multitasking can reduce productivity by 40%?[19] As surprising as this number is, even more surprising is that those who multitask believe that they are more productive than those focusing on one task. So let's have a closer look at multitasking.

The first thing to consider is that no one can truly multitask. What multitaskers are doing is "task switching." According to Guy Winch,[20] our brains have a finite amount of attention and productivity. If one is task switching, then saving time is by batching your tasks. For instance, schedule meetings on the same day if you need to attend meetings. This way, you get into the necessary mindset required for meetings and get them done at once (or in chunks of time). This approach is much better than having one meeting every day.

Switching frequently between tasks can also introduce errors in your work. This fact is especially relevant if your job involves a lot of critical thinking. For instance, a French study[21] concluded that while the human brain can handle two complicated tasks without too much trouble, introducing the third task can overwhelm the frontal cortex and increase mistakes.

Another reason not to multitask is that it increases stress. For example, the University of California found that employees who received a steady email stream stayed in a perpetual "high alert" mode with higher heart rates. Conversely, those without constant access multitasked less and were also less stressed.

Multitasking also increases "inattentional blindness." One study found that 75% of college students who walked across a street while talking on their cell phones did not notice a clown riding a unicycle nearby. Thus, since the brain did not register seeing the clown, there is a real danger of inattentional blindness. What if a speeding car was heading toward you while you were engaged on your cell phone?

Multitasking makes it harder to switch between tasks. This inability is especially true as our brains age. Another study[22] from the University of California in San Francisco concluded that it becomes harder to get back on track after interruptions. Sudden interruptions force us to focus on another task, thereby disrupting short-term memory.

All of this begs the question, *"Do those who say they can multitask actually multitask, and do they do it well?"* According to a University of Utah study,[23] you are much worse at multitasking than those who only engage in occasional multitasking if you engage in multitasking frequently.

STOP the next time you feel the need to bounce around between tasks. Instead, prioritize and schedule your work to focus on one task at a time. To become more productive, do not divide your attention between tasks. Consequently, frequent multitasking or task switching does more harm than good.

REFLECTION	• Are you a good multitasker? What makes you say that? • The next time you get multiple jobs/projects at once, how would you handle them? • What advice would you give multitaskers?

The Problem with Problems

Have you ever had one of those days when everything seems to be a problem? For example, your children are late for school, you miss the bus, and as you arrive at work, you realize that you forgot your meeting notes at home or, even worse, your shirt is stained. On top of that, two of your employees call in sick, and before you can browse your email inbox, your spouse calls asking if you can pick up your son from school because he's sick. OMG, right?

If you determine that the above scenario qualifies as a problem(s) (i.e., one of "those" days!), you are using what experts call "deficit thinking." By focusing on problems, our action plans will be concerned with fixing the problem or correcting the "deficit." We can see this kind of thinking in our personal lives and organizations.

Consider this: If we spend most of our time focusing on what is wrong with our organization, we can overlook what is right. And every organization has a mix of right and wrong. But organizations that look at what is right or working well can shift their concerns to create more opportunities for success.

This "appreciative inquiry" approach energizes, motivates, and helps organizations emphasize their strengths rather than weaknesses. In contrast, deficit thinking zaps our energy, de-motivates, and when we only focus on problems, we only see flaws. This approach does not say that organizations should ignore the issues or that problems will disappear through appreciative inquiry. On the contrary, organizations must resolve issues as they arise. If not, they can multiply like viruses. Thus, there is a time and place for appreciative inquiry and deficit thinking, with the latter beneficial for immediate resolutions.

There are several things that organizations can do to fix problems. The most important thing, however, is to distinguish problems from symptoms. If one works on correcting symptoms, then the problem never goes away. For example, kids being late for school, missing the bus, forgetting your meeting notes, or putting on the wrong shirt are the symptoms—the problem is that you didn't give yourself enough time to manage your morning.

Flipping the symptoms and problems on their heads, the fact that you ran late all morning gave you more time to spend with your children. Now that's an opportunity worth cherishing.

In addition to the appreciative inquiry versus deficit thinking approaches to problems, another way to frame our "problems" is to use the 90–10 Principle.[24] This principle says that we control 90% of what happens in our lives because of our choices. We can choose to rush through life or take a leisurely pace. We can choose to react in anger when something goes wrong or look on the bright side.

The problem with problems isn't a problem at all. Instead, it's an opportunity to grow personally and improve organizational effectiveness, which helps us learn innovative ways of handling problems. And in so doing, you might discover that you will have fewer problems to solve in the long term.

REFLECTION

- What are your biggest problems right now?
- What choices will help resolve your problems?
- What long-term action items will help you lessen the number of your problems?
- Can you avoid any problems altogether? How?
- What opportunities do you see in your problems?
- Does appreciative inquiry have a place in your life (e.g., work, school, home, family, etc.)? How would you use appreciative inquiry in these areas (if at all)?

Managing Energy to Manage Time

Did you know that the higher your energy, the better your time management ability? Therefore, since there are no limits on our energy, we can use our energy within the available time to produce more. The trick is in understanding our limitations on available energy. Let me explain.

Each of us reacts to emotional and physical stimuli differently. Some things energize us, while other things de-energize. For example, my energy soars when I identify the cause of a problem that inhibits efficiency. Then I get creative in identifying solutions. Conversely, my energy depletes when I work on mundane and repetitive tasks. Others might find the opposite effect.

When your energy soars, it's like your battery recharges—a sudden burst of energy makes you feel more enthusiastic, more capable, and better able to cope with whatever comes your way. The exciting thing about this "recharged" feeling is that it enables you to do more in less time. Subsequently, we can sustain this feeling by caring for ourselves to ensure optimum energy levels.

Here's how to recharge and sustain energy levels for maximum productivity.

1. Exercise regularly. Every day, schedule time for at least 30 minutes of moderate to vigorous exercise. Go for a walk, run, lift weights, and do whatever is necessary to wake up your body.

2. Determine your energy cycle. For three days, keep a log of your energy levels. For every hour (from the time you wake up until the

time you go to bed), rate your energy level from 0 (lowest) to 5 (highest). Review your log at the end of three days and identify your peak energy levels.

3. Use your peak energy levels to work on the most important, most challenging, and most focused work. When we do this, our productivity increases dramatically.

4. Create your perfect day. Use your peak energy levels to work on long-range and interim goals, choosing tasks to achieve your goals. Schedule and work on low-energy tasks during your non-peak energy times.

5. Manage yourself every day to achieve your career and personal goals. Unfortunately, there is no magic or quick solution for this. You will get out of your day what you put into your day.

In addition to the above, make time for fun activities to boost your energy. How about lunch with your BFF or playing a Scrabble or Words with Friends game? Or what about taking your boss for coffee to discuss your career strategy as the perfect energizer?

Whatever you do, use your energy wisely and boost it. When you do, your mood will be lighter, and you will get everything done more effectively and efficiently. In addition, it will feel like you have more hours in your day. That's the result of managing ourselves to boost our energy.

REFLECTION

- What time of day do you experience your peak energy level?
- To what do you devote your time during your daily peak energy level? Is that a good use of your time? Explain.
- Do you maintain a regular exercise routine? If not, will you commit to doing so starting now? Tip: Your health is super important in keeping you in top form to manage anything thrown your way during the day. Stay healthy to stay energized.

The Key to Productivity

Do you remember the last time you faced a task you didn't enjoy? Do you remember what you did? The chances are that if you completed the task, you started working on it and didn't stop until you finished the job.

"Starting" is the key to productivity.

When you have difficulty starting, the task waits. If the wait is excessive, you may work under pressure to finish the job. This approach is not a good way to work since working under pressure creates more stress for you and others. It also increases the chances for mistakes since the tight timeline leaves little room to correct things that may go wrong. When you work under pressure like this, you almost always produce an inferior product.

There are many reasons people have difficulty getting started with tasks, but here are some considerations to help you push yourself to start.

1. If you resist starting on that project because you feel your outcome may not be what you expect, remember that risk is inherent in everything we do. And even if you fail to achieve your result, you will have a valuable learning experience.

2. Is overwhelm your enemy? Break up the overwhelming task into small manageable tasks. Then start working on the small pieces, one at a time, until completion. Breaking the task into small parts helps alleviate overwhelm.

3. “Paralysis by analysis” applies to those who need everything to be perfect. As a result, they may never start the task. To help you overcome this perfectionist approach, just start! Just starting will create the momentum needed to follow through on the task.

4. When boredom creeps into your work, you will avoid doing the work. Unfortunately, this avoidance only creates more work because we work on our “waiting” pile when our energy is lowest. To overcome boredom, just start on the task. The sooner you finish, the sooner you can return to more exciting work.

5. Do you enjoy working under pressure? If so, you probably put things off until the last minute. This delay creates more stress not only for you but also for others. It also increases the chances for mistakes, leaving no time for their correction. Working under pressure almost always results in a mediocre product. Give yourself time for the task and start working on it on time, not at the last minute.

6. Use good time management techniques like the above to push yourself to be more productive. When you do, you will notice a considerable gain in free time in your days. That’s something worth starting, isn’t it?

Being productive means having more time to do the things you truly love. Therefore, by improving your productivity, you will acquire more time.

REFLECTION

- What type of work do you enjoy doing? Why?
- What type of work do you detest? Why?
- What do you do to avoid starting a job you dislike? How could you incorporate your avoidance strategy into starting the disliked job?
- Do you work well under pressure? Note: Some people can work well under pressure, but the problem is *always* working under pressure. If you tend to work frequently under pressure (e.g., leaving jobs until the last minute), give yourself a break and schedule your tasks to relieve some stress. Your body and mind will thank you.
- How can you avoid leaving jobs until the last minute? What can you do to provide a more balanced working environment for yourself and others?

Not all Priorities are Created Equal

Many clients ask me how I juggle so many competing priorities—they think I'm always multitasking. My response is that not all priorities are the same, and you can only work on one focus at any time. Let me explain.

If you feel you have many priorities that need to get done at once, you know it is impossible to do them all simultaneously, let alone do them all well. So what is the solution? The solution is to prioritize your tasks based on their long-term importance and short-term urgency. The goal is to focus first on those tasks that are important. Then evaluate the "urgent" tasks to determine the true nature of their urgency. You may be surprised at how few urgent tasks are urgent—some may also have little importance.

Writing your tasks allows you to see them in front of you and provides an opportunity for their evaluation. Also, you get them out of your head by writing things—this eases the burden of "mental clutter." For example, here's a simple "priority matrix"[25] to consider.

Task	**Importance (Long Timeframe)**	**Urgency (Short Timeframe)**	**Total Score**	**Priority Score**

Here is how to use the matrix:

1. At the end of each day, list all the tasks you need to do tomorrow.

2. For each task, assign a rating for importance and urgency ranging from one to three, as follows:

   1 = high importance or urgency (i.e., not completing the task has severe consequences)
   2 = medium importance or urgency (i.e., not completing the task results in consequences, but you can manage the consequences without too much effort)
   3 = low importance or urgency (i.e., not completing the task won't create significant problems for anyone)

3. Add up each row's importance and urgency to get a "Total."

4. Now rank your tasks under "priority" by using the number in the total column. The category with the LOWEST TOTAL is your #1 Priority. You must do it FIRST.

Here is an example of the completed matrix:

Task	**Importance (Long Timeframe)**	**Urgency (Short Timeframe)**	**Total Score**	**Priority Score**
Meet with Barb to finalize the department's budget	1	1	2	1
Review marketing plan	2	2	4	3
Review operations plan	2	2	4	3

Task	Importance (Long Timeframe)	Urgency (Short Timeframe)	Total Score	Priority Score
Meet with Donna, and review applications for the vacant position	2	3	5	4
Attend weekly departmental meeting	3	1	4	3
Lunch with a prospective client	1	3	4	3
Prepare training outline	3	3	6	5
Prepare briefing note re: environmental claim	1	1	2	1
Prepare service plan for input to the strategic plan	2	1	3	2
Organize departmental strategic planning session	1	2	3	2

What is evident in the matrix is that several priorities have the same rank (e.g., four tasks show up with priority 3). When this occurs, take the competing priorities and re-prioritize them against each other until you end up with a list of priorities you can handle one at a time.

For instance:

Task	Importance (Long Timeframe)	Urgency (Short Timeframe)	Total Score	Priority Score
Meet with Barb to finalize the department's budget	1	1	2	1
Prepare briefing note re: environmental claim	1	1	2	1
Prepare service plan for input to the strategic plan	2	1	3	2
Organize departmental strategic planning session	1	2	3	2
Review marketing plan	2	2	4	3
Review operations plan	2	2	4	3
Attend weekly departmental meeting	3	1	4	3
Lunch with a prospective client	1	3	4	3
Meet with Donna, and review applications for the vacant position	2	3	5	4
Prepare training outline	3	3	6	5

If this cannot occur, ask your boss (or client, as the case may be) which priority comes first. For instance, in the above, we see two items as the number one priority with high importance and urgency (*meet with Barb to finalize the department's budget and prepare briefing note re: environmental claim*). Which one should you do? First, decide and then delegate the other high-priority item. By delegating work, you can complete it on time. Prioritizing your work comes down to your ability to plan your day and stick to your plan!

You may be looking at this matrix and thinking, "why should I waste my time developing a matrix like this to plan out my next day when prioritizing like this takes more time—time that I do not have?" That's a great question! Here is my response:

You will save three hours in execution for every hour you spend planning.

Therefore, prioritizing and working on your number one priority each day pays in saved time, efficiency, and productivity.

However, I'd like to add a disclaimer here: If a task takes you only a few minutes to complete, do not write it in the matrix. In other words, if it takes you longer to write what you need to do than it does to do it, then as the saying goes, just do it!

REFLECTION

- How do you go about determining your top priorities for your workday? Is your method working well for you?
- Would you be willing to try a different method to help you prioritize your day's work? Explain.
- Whatever method you use to organize your day, be sure it enables your productivity and saves you time in the process.

The Little Things ARE Important

When we focus on getting things done, we typically focus on allotting time for the essential and time-consuming tasks. If it's vital and will take a long time, we must get it done first, right? Yes and no.

When prioritizing, it is easy to forget to take care of the quick work—which we can complete in a minute or two—regardless of its importance. When we consistently defer the little things, they can become big things, and big things can be much harder to manage. The difficulty is that when we face a mountain of big things, we can become overwhelmed, which may lead to procrastination, leading to more little things piling up and becoming big things. It becomes a vicious cycle—little work becomes considerable, leading to overwhelm, procrastination, and more extensive work. This cycle can lead to stress that eventually leads to poor health.

Take email as an example. How many emails do you have in your email inbox (count those you opened and are still in your inbox - be honest with your counting)? Take note: any number above zero is too many. Why? Because as soon as you open an email, you should take action to remove it from your inbox. If you open an email and leave it in your inbox (whether or not you acted on it), the accumulating open emails in your inbox become electronic clutter contributing to mental clutter and overwhelm.

For email management, follow the B-F-A-T rule: Bring forward the items that you cannot answer right away, File items that are completed or do not require action, Act on items that require attention, and Toss items that need no further action or provide no value to your or your organization's work.

For any task that you can do within a couple of minutes, do it immediately. If you do, you will decrease your workload almost instantaneously. You will also reduce your mental clutter. The goal is to start working on tasks that can get done quickly and complete them. In other words—if you start, don't stop until completion.

Any tasks that keep nagging, such as unpaid bills, unmade appointments, or unfiled papers—all of these things can take less than a few minutes, but as soon as you get them done, you are saving yourself from carrying them in your head as a "need to do."

If you have thought about something more than once but have not taken action to complete it, this is an item that you must take care of immediately, especially if you can get it done in a few minutes.

A little-known side-effect of doing quick tasks right away is that not stopping something you start can translate to developing good habits. For instance, if you know you need to go for a workout (the thought keeps nagging you), putting on your runners (starting) will take less than a minute. Then, once you've got them on, follow through on the task (don't stop).

Whether at work or home, turn nagging thoughts into actions and start working on all the little things to completion. When you do, the inertia of your efforts will result in good habits that can last a lifetime.

All you need is to get started.

REFLECTION

- How many "**opened**" emails do you have right now in your email inbox?
- How will you handle these opened emails in your inbox right now?
- How will you handle your email going forward?
- Incorporate "BFAT" into your daily routine, and you will notice a tremendous difference in time savings with your email.
- How many small tasks can you accomplish today to leave time for more significant work?
- You've got this!

Controlling Time

A search on Amazon.ca on January 18, 2022, returned 3.24 billion hits on books on time management. The prevalence of these resources indicates that we have a problem understanding how to manage our time.

Psychology Today defines time management as the "ability to plan and control how you spend the hours in your day to effectively accomplish your goals." In short, if you don't set goals, you will likely have time management problems. But research also shows that even those who set goals can struggle with time. So perhaps the question we need to address is not how to manage time but how individuals need to organize themselves to achieve their goals, if indeed achieving goals is the (pardon the pun) goal.

How are you managing yourself? Does your typical day start with checking email and then tweeting about last night's events? Do you browse social media to catch up on what your hundreds of friends did over the weekend? Or do you review the list you created last night outlining your priorities for today? In the first instance, you allow technology and others to manage your time. In the latter instance, you are in control. Controlling yourself and your time means that you:

- Plan your day(s).
- Identify the important and urgent tasks and do them first.
- Build in "free time" in your plan to allow yourself to relax.
- Stick to your plan, only sidetracking for emergencies.

- Update your plan after emergencies to get back on track.
- Say no to work or non-work activities that add no value to you or your organization's strategic direction.
- Build relationships that will enable you to accomplish your tasks/goals.

Let's face it: No amount of instruction on time management will help you manage your time if you allow events or people to control your time. Only *you* can control *yourself,* including making and following through on decisions that will propel you to achieve your goals.

How you control yourself dictates how you manage your time. We all have the same amount of time on any day—1,440 minutes exactly. So control how you use each minute daily by building good habits. If you do, you'll never again need advice on time management.

REFLECTION

- How do you start each day? Is this effective for you? Explain.
- If your circumstances were ideal, how would you start your day? What can you do to realize this perfect start to your day?
- How do you manage your time when others impede your time? How could you manage your time in these situations?
- Visualize your ideal workday. How can you make it happen?

Triage – Best Served Regularly

Triage helps us decipher between the important and unimportant and ensures we do the right work at the right time and to/for the right person/thing. But be aware: Avoid the trap of triaging work just to keep workflow moving.

Blindly triaging work can cost more than stopping the flow to challenge whether the work is necessary in the first place. This challenge is particularly relevant to writing reports that no one will ever read, creating programs that no one will ever use, or creating new departments with limited (or no) usefulness to stakeholders or the organization. Of course, you have an obligation to your organization to challenge when your work has no value. But if you are doing the right work and for the right reasons, managing work through triage can be very effective.

Triage is about prioritizing work based on its importance and urgency. It is beneficial when applied to managing information. For example, you can save time by triaging information such as correspondence and email if the most important gets done first. Many might say that triage is like applying the 80:20 rule to everything you do—you create 80% of your results from 20% of your efforts by focusing on the important and urgent.

How do you determine what is important and urgent? Here are five suggestions for dispatching your important and urgent work to create superb results for you and your organization:

1. Keep an updated "to-do" list and focus on completing the medium-important, high urgency goals most of the time. This method

will give you 80% of your results. Next, constantly scan your list and drop items of low importance or those with no urgency.

2. Standardize work whenever you can. For instance, have procedures for writing reports, formatting documents, handling email, etc. The more standards in your organization, the more time you will have for high-productivity and high-creativity items instead of re-inventing procedures each time you need to write a report, format a document, or respond to an email.

3. When making decisions, don't focus on the decision. Instead, focus on options that may result in the right decision. It's much easier to decide based on a few options instead of making a decision based on the entire case.

4. Close your email and browser when working on important work. You will get the essential tasks done much sooner.

5. Stop multitasking. Multitasking is counterproductive. Everyone's brain slows down considerably when trying to juggle multiple tasks.

If the above still falls short of helping you and your organization achieve efficient workflow, outsourcing work is another option. Hiring experts costs much less than fumbling through work not within your organization's area of expertise.

The fact is that none of us are good at everything, but all of us are good at something. So, ultimately, determine the areas where you and your organization create the most value. Then outsource everything else.

REFLECTION

- Do you have a standardized method for completing frequently occurring tasks (e.g., pre-formatted templates, automatically-inserted signature lines, etc.)? If not, consider creating standardized methods where it makes sense to do so to improve your workflow.
- What are you good at—really good at—that you could take that strength and apply it to your job or career? How can you capitalize on your strengths to enable efficiency in your workflow?
- What is your approach to decision-making? Is your method effective, or could it use some tweaking? How could you tweak your process?

Changing Culture: One Person at a Time

Culture includes group norms of behavior and the underlying shared values that help keep those norms in place. For example, look at the typical meetings in your office. Is everyone on time, or do meetings usually start five, ten, or more minutes later than scheduled? What about attention to detail? Do final project reports receive a thorough review and commentary or are they filed as received, never to see the light of day again? These scenarios all represent organizational culture.

If your employees are stressed, overwhelmed, or procrastinate on deadlines, or if your company is always underperforming, don't blame your employees. Instead, look at your organization's leaders. An organization's leaders or founders establish values that permeate and manifest in behaviors. The more these behaviors loop back to the leaders' values, the more they are reinforced and perpetuated throughout the organization.

Leaders must change their values and behaviors to change an organization's culture. They can do this by creating a vision for the company and explaining how working toward the vision will help its employees grow. In addition, leaders need to be persuasive and model the behavior they wish to see from their employees, frequently engaging in conversations with all staff to "sell" the vision and inspire them. This approach is the correct one.

An incorrect approach to changing organizational culture is through disincentives such as coercion, threats, or punishment. These "power tools" may incite change in employees' or departmental behaviors, but the change is temporary at best. At worst, it ruins staff morale and results in high staff turnover. Therefore, using power tools to influence cultural change is not sustainable or desirable.

Here are four considerations for changing your organization's culture to one that is efficient, productive, and effective:

1. Sell the new vision by enlisting early adopters and those on the fence to join you in selling the vision. Once they do, ensure that you recognize them for their accomplishments.

2. Don't just preach about the need for change. Instead, use examples from your company to demonstrate an urgency for change. For instance, have managers take calls from disgruntled customers to understand why customers cancel orders at the last minute, leaving the company in the red by thousands of dollars for each product design prototype not purchased.

3. Redistribute resources to the 20% of areas that produce 80% of the company's results. These are areas where implementing change first will have a tremendous positive impact organization-wide.

4. Enlist an individual in your company called a "consigliere" (*source: Blue Ocean Strategy*). This individual will find out who is fighting change, who supports change, and what you need to do to build strategies for sustainable change.

To this last point, a stumbling block to any change initiative is typically an "old guard" mentality that is steadfastly held, usually by long-time employees.

Therefore, leaders must spend much time with these individuals to help them buy into the organization's vision and not disrupt the new way forward.

Changing an organization's culture is probably one of the leaders' most challenging responsibilities. It's a slow process, but the rewards of working in a dynamic company where respect and appreciation of everyone's time are top of mind will go a long way to ensuring long-term organizational and personal success.

REFLECTION

- How would you describe your organization's culture?
- How do you feel about your organization's culture?
- Are your organization's leaders enablers of a positive culture? If not, what could they do differently to move toward a positive culture?
- How can you contribute to improving your organization's culture? Will you do it?

The Good and Bad of Habits

Habits allow us not to "think" about what we are doing; they're an automatic response to stimuli. Therefore, they can be helpful when we are engaged in rote or mundane activities like getting up in the morning, showering, or cleaning the house. Because we don't have to think about these activities, we can do them quickly and free our minds to think about other things such as planning our day.

While habits can help speed up some activities, they can also inhibit success. If you examine your life's results and are honest with yourself, you can quickly attribute your results to your habits. For instance, some habits create stress: procrastination, consistently neglecting your promises, handling work more than once (i.e., keep shuffling your "to-do's" to the back of the pile consistently), or saving opened emails in your inbox. With repetition of bad habits, stress compounds to create even more stress.

Research shows that up to 90% of our behaviors are habits. However, research also shows that we can modify our habits in as little as 12 weeks. While the reasons why we engage in self-defeating patterns can be as varied as the individuals themselves, there are ways to get on the track to success. Here are the steps you can take to eliminate your bad habits:

1. Identify your negative habits. Write them on paper or in a Word document or other application and have a good look at them.

2. Select one habit that you wish to improve. (Yes, only one!).

3. Identify behaviors that will replace the one habit you selected.

4. Start practicing the new behavior(s) every day and keep practicing it for at least three months until it becomes a habit. Use reminders to help with this by placing post-it notes in locations you can't miss, using pop-up reminders/alarms in your email calendar, or engaging others to assist you (e.g., coaching, telephone, other reminders, etc.).

5. Commit to a "no exceptions" rule to stay on track with your new habit.

The last item, committing to a no-exceptions rule, is essential. Your efforts may not pay off if you decide to waver even slightly. Imagine if organizations chose to be "flexible" with their policies and procedures and allowed some exceptions, claiming that 99.9% is good enough. With a 99.9% "good enough" rate, you would get, for example, one hour of unsafe drinking water per month, two dangerous landings at major airports each day, and doctors around the country dropping 50 newborn babies at birth every day. I'm sure you'll agree that none of these scenarios is acceptable, even if they account for only 0.1% of instances.

If you replace one bad habit with a new behavior every three months, you will acquire four new positive habits each year. This acquisition translates to at least four steps closer to a more prosperous life—whatever success may be for you.

REFLECTION

- What does a successful life mean to you?
- What steps will you take to achieve a successful life?
- What one "bad" habit has been nagging you for a while? What can you do to replace that habit with a new positive one?

Leaving is Sometimes the Only Way to Send a Message

It was one of those days. You have a lot of work to get through. You have everything slotted, prioritized, sorted, itemized, allocated, dissected, trisected, and placed like a well-oiled machine. Then it happens: the one appointment in your day where you wait, wait, and wait some more. It occurred to me recently.

Those who believe in and rely on schedules and priorities to make our lives flow smoothly have no room or patience for those who abuse our valuable time. My week was going very well, meetings held, appointments kept, errands accomplished; generally, everything flowed as it should until a medical appointment made me stop.

I won't use the doctor's name, but he is an ophthalmologist in my town. My appointment was at 1:30 p.m., and the receptionist told me I would need a driver since the doctor would dilate my eyes. No problem. I arranged for a driver and arrived for my appointment a few minutes before the scheduled time.

When I arrived, a couple of people were in the waiting room, so I took a seat and waited. And waited. And waited. At 2:00 p.m., I went to the receptionist and asked if I'd be seeing the doctor soon, given that my appointment was for 1:30 p.m. She wasn't sure, but she assured me that it wouldn't be too long.

A few minutes after 2:00 p.m., an office technician called my name and took me to a room where we spent about 10 minutes running some eye tests. Then it was down the hall where I entered another waiting area because no exam room was available.

At 2:30 p.m., the lady took me into an exam room and told me that the doctor would be in shortly. I'm not sure what "shortly" means to her, but when I hear "shortly," I think within about five minutes, with a stretch, maybe ten minutes. So again, I waited, somewhat patiently. However, at 2:50 p.m., I left the exam room and stopped at the receptionist's desk to tell her I was leaving. I told her I felt it was disrespectful of the doctor to waste my time. I reminded her that my appointment was at 1:30 p.m., and I waited much longer than I should have, almost 90 minutes with no doctor in sight. In my book, it just doesn't work that way.

I vowed to never return to that clinic, but a happy footnote caught me by surprise. That evening, the doctor in question telephoned and apologized for my wait. Ironically, his process and workflow predicament got snagged during my appointment time, and as the *Queen of Lean*, I didn't let him off the hook that easily.

Simple fixes like ensuring reception staff communicate correct information pre and during appointment times will improve customer (patient) relationships and shorten wait times. After that, we'll need to work on helping the doctor process his patients more efficiently. The result will be a win-win for all with no accumulated patient backlog. Happy patients. Happy doctor. Happy staff. Who can argue with that?

REFLECTION

- Do you have a similar "waiting" experience? How did it make you feel? How did you handle it?
- Do your clients/customers ever wait on you for something? If so, what is the cause of the delay? How can you improve the wait time?
- Improving processes can go a long way to improving time management, resulting in good customer relations.

Ignoring the Important Creates Crises

I keep coming back to lists. Complete lists, i.e., writing *all* the things that need doing. Whether things need doing now, next week, next month, or next year, they must be on your list. Why? Because if they're not on a list, there is a good chance that you will forget about them, and when that happens, you have a crisis on your hands.

If you're "fighting fires" regularly at work, it's not because the crisis suddenly arose (granted, sometimes there are actual crises, but these are few and far between, thankfully). Instead, the situation occurs because you completed higher priority items while ignoring the critical items. So the essential things simmered, then boiled out of control to create a crisis.

I have been in many organizations where the attitude toward dealing with undesirable (or less important) work is to "ignore it, and it'll go away." Well, the fact is, work doesn't go away. It comes back and keeps coming back until someone completes the work. That's why it's called "work."

There are many advantages to keeping lists. For example, lists help with the following:

1. Improved memory. When you write things, you get them out of your head. Think about this: our short-term memory can only hold about seven things simultaneously. With each successive "thing" kept in short-term memory, the ability to hold onto it diminishes. You're setting yourself up for failure if you have more than seven things to do and don't have a list.

2. Improved productivity. Lists help you focus your energy on tasks without the distraction of juggling to-do items in your head. Without lists, your mind works harder than it needs to, but with lists, you gain sharper focus and improve your productivity.

3. Improved organization. Without question, this is a crucial reason to make lists. Lists help you plan your time so that you work more efficiently. For example, spending 15 minutes on planning gives you an hour saved.

4. Increased motivation. Lists help you to clarify goals. When this occurs, you gain inspiration to work toward your goals. And each time you accomplish a goal and strike it off your list, your motivation improves even more.

5. Reduced stress. By prioritizing all to-do's, you give things a place in your life rather than your mind, thus reducing stress.

There are several online tracking (to-do) templates; however, I have not tried them. I keep my lists in my email calendar because that's how I work best. In contrast, you may find another format better for your work. For example, some people use Excel spreadsheets. Regardless of format, the key is to include due dates (and start dates) based on priority and how long each task will require. You might consider applying project management principles to help you with this aspect of your list.

Update your list with all your to-do's. Then get ready to be more productive, organized, motivated, have better memory, reduce stress, and acquire more time in your life. I don't know about you, but keeping lists sounds like a "no-brainer" to me. So, where's your to-do list?

REFLECTION

- Do you have a to-do list? If not, will you give it a try?
- To prioritize your activities, try using a time management matrix (discussed in "Not all Priorities are Created Equal" in this book).
- Remember only to include more significant items in your to-do list. Don't include tasks you can do in a couple of minutes—do those immediately to get them off your desk.

Workflow as Easy as P-D-S-A

In 1939, Walter Shewhart introduced "plan-do-check-act" as a scientific process of acquiring knowledge. In the 1980s, Edwards Deming refined the cycle by changing "check" into a "study" process. The cycle is logical, and one can use it to test information before moving to the next step. We can apply it to learning and improving our daily workflow to save time. Here's how.

Plan

- Write everything that you need to do. Then, hold this list in your in-basket, notebook, email folder, or calendar—where you usually keep your "to-do's" (but not in your head).
- Review the items on your list and determine priorities.
- Determine resource requirements for each item on your list. Can you do it all yourself? Or do you need to delegate? To whom will you delegate?
- Do you need equipment or materials to complete work on any of the items on your list? Note what is required and when/where to order.
- How much time will you take to complete each item on your list? Then, when you have your timeline, multiply it by three to get a realistic timeline.
- Schedule time in your calendar for each planned item based on your realistic timeline.
- Remember to schedule priority items first—base priority on your organization's

requirements in light of long-term goals and objectives. If you're unsure what a priority item is, ask someone who knows the answer.

- When scheduling time to accomplish tasks, take into account your energy cycle. For instance, if your energy is higher in the morning, plan to work on more complex tasks, leaving less demanding work for the afternoon, such as returning phone calls or emails, attending meetings, etc.

Do

- Do the work as planned. In other words, work your plan!
- Follow B-F-A-T for email and everything else. For instance, if the scheduled item requires considerable work, B-bring it forward by scheduling time to work on it (e.g., big projects, research, report writing, etc.). If the item is for information purposes only, then F-file it. If you can deal with the thing in less than two minutes, then A-act on it now. If the item has no value to you or the organization, T-toss/delete it. There. You're done.

Study

- Daily, weekly, and monthly, review your calendar and list of to-dos.
- Update your to-do list by deleting complete items and rescheduling items that allow rescheduling.
- Keep your list current.
- If you're falling behind schedule, can you delegate work? On the other hand, perhaps your timelines are inaccurate. In this case, re-examine your estimates, requirements, and priorities.

- What modifications do you need to make to your priorities, schedule, resources, timelines, delegated work, etc.?

Act

- Make adjustments to your work plan based on the review of your work (i.e., the "study" phase).
- Go back to the "plan" phase and repeat the cycle.

You may have noticed this four-step process because we spend the most time in the planning phase. This time expenditure makes sense because planning is the most crucial part of anything. If we don't plan, we set ourselves up for failure. It is not unusual to spend up to 80% of our time planning. Executing is relatively easy once you know what you need to do and you're prepared by planning for it.

Repeat this cycle as frequently as you need. You can do this several times, even within one task. This cycle is the key to continuous improvement in your workflow.

Imagine if each individual used a continuous improvement cycle in their work. The resulting benefits would include organization-wide continuous improvements such as greater efficiency, greater productivity, less waste, and a culture that thrives on innovation and change. Thus, the plan-do-study-act cycle is your key to continuing success.

REFLECTION

- When you plan your work for the day, do you skip to "doing" without planning first? How is that working for you?
- When you work, do you do it efficiently or just do what you're told?
- When you complete your work, do you ever review how you might have done it more efficiently and saved yourself some time in the process? This review of completed work is a great way to glean lessons learned for similar future work.

Success is Twenty Percent Intelligent Effort

For the longest time, I was doing it all wrong. First, I was killing myself with work. Then, adding insult to injury, I was doing the wrong work. I use "wrong" to indicate that I focused on everything rather than zeroing in on the most important thing. Then, finally, I think exhaustion made me stop. That was when I realized that perhaps Pareto was right.

In 1906, Wilfredo Pareto, an Italian economist, observed that 20% of the population in Italy owned 80% of the land and that 20% of the pea pods in his garden contained 80% of the peas and other similar observations. In 1941, Joseph Juran, a management consultant, applied Pareto's observations to quality issues, coining the Pareto Principle: the "law of the vital few and trivial many" (or, as Juran preferred, "law of the vital few and useful many") which states that 80% of the effects come from 20% of the causes.

Considering this, 80% of our results come from 20% of our efforts. The flip side is also true: 20% of our results can come from 80% of our efforts. In the first instance, you're working on the important; in the second, you're not. Many individuals don't rise above the bar; instead, they devote 80% of their efforts to producing a mere 20% results. But those few that do rise above do so because they've mastered the art of work.

Working is essential for good health, happiness, and wealth (i.e., 20% effort for an 80% result). But if you're spending most of your time working on things that don't matter, you're probably working to the detriment of your good health, happiness, and wealth (i.e., 80% effort for a 20% result). Who doesn't want to work less, get the same or better results, and have more free time? I know I do.

Over the past several months, I've heard complaints about the long hours people spend at work, but without the reciprocal results for their effort. Consequently, I ask them how much time they spend each week working on their strategy or priority projects to put this into perspective. Then I ask them how much time they spend socializing (or checking social media, watching television, or gaming). Enough said.

What drives success? It's not the amount of effort or long hours you put into your work. Success is about using efficient systems and processes to work less on everything and more on the important. First, think about where you're wasting your time. Now think about how you could use that time on important tasks to acquire time to waste without guilt.

Here's to your success.

REFLECTION

- What's your biggest time waster? How is that impacting your important work?
- Where do you spend most of your time at work? At home? Is this appropriate?
- Where would you like to spend most of your time? How will you modify your daily habits to spend most of your time where you want?

Relax to Gain Power

Talking about time management without touching on productivity is difficult because those with good time management capabilities are more productive. In addition, productivity is directly proportional to your ability to control stress. The more you control your stress, the better your time management and vice versa. In addition, the more you can manage your stress, the greater your productivity, and with greater productivity comes greater power.

Imagine this:

- Your boss has moved the reporting deadline forward
- You need to pick up your kids from school
- Your in-laws are coming for dinner this weekend
- The project team meeting requires rescheduling
- The house needs cleaning
- You need to buy groceries
- A key project team member called in sick today
- The piano teacher canceled the kids' piano lessons this week
- —and that's just from the top of your head!

Can you see the problem with this? The problem is that the to-do's that directly inhibit your productivity consume your mind. But it doesn't have to be this way. The constant rattling of "to-do's" in your head compromises your power and ability to relax. So what to do about this? Ideally, create systems that help to relax your mind.

When one has a system for managing their day, the mind quiets. And when the mind is quiet, you can approach your day and its challenges with the necessary focus. But when your mind is noisy, you cannot do this—the white noise zaps your power. So to stop the noise and take back your control, here are five things you can do right now:

1. Today, plan for tomorrow. In other words, today, make a list of everything you need to accomplish tomorrow.

2. Update your list. Take that list and input it into your calendar, scheduling sufficient time for each to-do.

3. Manage too many to-dos. Too many to-dos for tomorrow? Bounce non-priority items to the next day and the days after that. Tomorrow's to-dos are only "must do tomorrow" things, not "must do this week/month" items.

4. Manage yourself and your work habits. Be honest with yourself. Are you following your schedule? If not, where are you wasting your time and why? Identify timewasters and get rid of them.

5. Control your work environment. You can manage external distractions, including telephone calls, emails, visitors, and a noisy work environment.

When I schedule all my activities and follow them, my mind is free to focus only on the immediate task on which I'm working. Why? Because I trust that my system will alert me when the next task or meeting is due. I don't have to worry about upcoming tasks in the meantime. The freedom gained using schedules and lists is in the productivity gains that naturally occur from this freedom.

You owe yourself to free your mind and take back your power. Of course, the increased productivity you will experience will make you shine at work, feel better, and be more fun to be around. And who wouldn't want this experience?

REFLECTION

- Do you schedule time in your calendar today for work the next day? It's a great habit – try it if you aren't already doing this.
- How do you get back on track when you slip from your schedule? Does this work well for you?
- How do you manage external distractions? Is your method working well, or do you need to revisit the methodology?
- Remember that it's best to ask for assistance if something feels overwhelming rather than let it simmer and get out of control.

It's Not Sex or Drinking: It's Stress, and It's Soaring[26]

A study in 2012 found that six in ten workers in major global economies are experiencing increased workplace stress. China (75%) has the highest rise in workplace stress.[27] In addition, the *American Institute of Stress* reports that 80% of workers feel pressure on the job, and nearly half say they need help to learn how to manage stress. In addition, 42% say their co-workers need such help.

A more recent study in 2019 in the United States found that nearly three in five employees (59%) experienced negative impacts of work-related stress in the past month, including a lack of interest, motivation, or energy (26%), difficulty focusing (21%), and a lack of effort at work (19%).[28]

What is causing all this stress?

One of the leading causes of stress is the complexity found in faster-better-more technology. Unfortunately, with the faster-better-more comes an inherent risk of inefficiency and ineffectiveness for those on the managing end. I submit that most companies have done a poor job of helping their staff manage technology.

Think about something as innocuous as email. How much stress do you incur due to too much email? Does your company provide you with resources, training, and guidance to help you manage your email so that it is not a source of stress for you (and those who attempt to communicate with you via email)?

Consider this: the Radicati Group predicts we will have 4.6 billion email accounts by 2025. Corporate email makes up 25% of these amounts yet accounts for most of the world's email traffic. In 2019, the average person received 126 emails daily; worldwide, daily emails received and sent were 205 billion.

By 2025, we will see about 377 billion emails sent daily.[29] On the other hand, experts expect consumer email to decrease due to the increased use of texting and other social media such as Facebook, LinkedIn, Twitter, Instagram, etc. In addition, mobile email is also growing.

It's no wonder that stress is soaring. Juggling the ineffectiveness and inefficiencies imposed by technology at work only to come home to even more of the same can increase stress. So how does one cope with this bombardment? Here are some suggestions to help you stop stress from soaring in your life:

1. Prepare for work by not rushing to work. Instead, give yourself lots of time to get there. Studies show that you will feel more stressed and less productive if you start your day rushing. Practicing good time management will help you stop rushing.

2. Keep your email inbox clear. Zero items at the end of the day is the rule, not a suggestion (for work and home email accounts). Immediately move all read items out of your inbox into appropriate storage locations (i.e., personal folders, shared drive folders, delete, print, file, etc.). By doing this, you will reduce your visual clutter and also be able to search for email items more efficiently.

3. Set priorities for your day and stick to those priorities. Unless there's an emergency, there's no reason to shift priorities. Shifting will only pull you behind schedule. Instead, you want to be ahead since you will experience less stress.

4. Go home on time whenever you can. Sometimes you may need to do overtime, but this should be the exception rather than the rule. Going home on time means you are sticking to a schedule. And this implies relaxation for you and your family about schedules.

5. Don't use your mobile devices or desktop computer at home until you've had a chance to unwind. Spend time with your family and enjoy dinner before checking your mobile devices. I check my mobile device only if I expect to hear from a friend or family member or if I want to get in touch with them. Otherwise, work can wait until the morning.

6. Get enough sleep. Sleep and efficiency go hand in hand. Decreasing sleep by as little as 1.5 hours for just one night reduces daytime alertness by 32%. In this example, your ability to function is about as good as someone intoxicated. Get at least 7.5–8.0 hours of sleep every night. Use time management planning and plan your bedtime, sticking to your regular bedtime routine every night. On-time.

Practice the above six steps, and you will be helping yourself reduce your stress. As a result, you will experience a better mood, better sleep, and less tension and anxiety; you will make fewer mistakes at work, gain better concentration, and be much happier.

REFLECTION

- How does stress impact your time? Some people seem to thrive on working under pressure, which can affect your health.
- Do you get enough sleep? I've heard people say that "sleep is for the weak." These people are entirely wrong. Sleep is for those that value their contributions to society and wish to improve their value daily. Get enough sleep to be a well-functioning human.
- How are you managing your email? Are you following the "BFAT" rule to clear every opened email item out of your inbox immediately? Remember BFAT = bring forward items you can't deal with immediately, file items that need no action, act on items that can get done quickly (a few minutes), and toss (delete) items that require no further action.
- How do you prepare for work? Are you scheduling the next day's work today? Are you prioritizing your tasks?

Just Thinking About It Won't Get You There

One of the things that I've discovered is that many people are great at planning, i.e., thinking about changing processes or producing better outcomes. However, they get stuck when reducing their plans to projects or actionable tasks. If you tend to fall in this group—spending your days thinking about what you need to get done but never seem to launch out of thinking mode—then read on. I've got good news for you.

Actionable lists can help you define your projects and move you from thinking about what needs to get done to identifying tasks that will get you there. Lists provide visual cues and reminders to do the work. However, writing things and being reminded to do them won't get you there, either. What if you forget to look at your list regularly? In this instance, you need schedules.

Schedules keep you on track. When you know what needs doing (from your action list), use your calendar (I use my email calendar) to schedule time into your day (every day) for every single thing that needs doing. Think of a schedule as a reminder of your action list.

When scheduling work on a project, try to schedule the same type of work at the same time of day. For example, if you need to provide a project update report to your boss, schedule it for the same time each week (or day). This regularity provides consistency in work, and you are more apt to do this task if it occurs regularly at the same time. The nice thing about consistent scheduling is that the more you do the same thing at the same time, there is a point at which you won't need to look at your schedule for reminders to do the work.

When working on tasks, work in short bursts. Typically, we tend to be very focused for the first 20 or last 20 minutes of the job. If you can focus intently on your work for those 20 minutes and then take a break (look away from your work—perhaps look out the window, make a phone call, review your email, anything other than the task you are working on), you will be more productive than if you slog at the job for hours. Using this short burst method, you will also develop better quality work.

For complex tasks, schedule them during times of the day when you are most alert. For example, if you're high energy in the morning, then work on your difficult tasks in the morning and leave your afternoons for other jobs that allow greater flexibility in deadlines.

What's on your action list this month? A better question may be: where is your list? Is your list physically (or electronically) written in a place where you can easily find it? Or are you thinking about it? Dump that list from your mind and create a schedule of your action items. Lists and schedules are your stepping stone to success, no matter your task.

REFLECTION

- Do you schedule your action items somewhere accessible or keep them in your head? If in your head, how can you motivate yourself to dump those lists from your head into paper/electronic format?
- Use schedules to manage your time more efficiently.

Involuntary Systems are the Key to Success

Have you ever thought about how many times your heart beats in a second, minute, hour, or day? Very few of us think about how our body functions, yet it is –balancing our internal systems to keep us alive.

We can draw a parallel between our involuntary bodily and "involuntary" organizational systems. For example, imagine telling your heart each time blood needs to pump or your lungs when it's time to breathe. These constant reminders would be a very inefficient way of managing our bodies. Moreover, it would be an all-consuming exercise leaving us with no time to do anything else. Likewise, with office or personal organization systems: if they are not "second nature" or "involuntary," we struggle with disorganization, stress, procrastination, overwhelm, and other symptoms that hinder our productivity.

An organized person knows (almost intuitively) their priorities, including finding information and managing their time. Each time they need to work on a priority item, they immediately know how to do their work. They do not create a new system(s) for prioritizing or getting organized. Instead, they have created efficient workflow systems, so they need little time to maintain or think about them—much like involuntary heartbeats.

Think about a records management system that includes filing cabinets stuffed with file folders and documents. The file folders are labeled, but there is no consistency in labeling or filing. Do you think this system is easy to use? No, it is not. And because it is not easy to use, you need to think about how and where you will file your documents each time you use the system. Unfortunately, this thinking takes up your time and energy and creates stress. On the other hand, an intuitively organized filing system enables you to file "automatically" and keep work flowing seamlessly.

Other examples include expedited invoice payments or patients' triage at medical clinics. Once the workflow process is set up, and procedures learned for each function, you no longer need to think about how to do something. Your approach and methods have enabled you to devise your automatic system for how you work. As a result, the work becomes second nature —the more automated the flow, the more organized the system.

A nice side effect of automatic processes and systems is that they enable us to be more creative. We do not have to think about the process or procedure; we just do our work. Like our heart beating in the background, our operations and systems are also in silent mode. This automation enables our minds the freedom to explore new opportunities, giving us the ability to be even more productive.

Next time you work on a task, ask yourself if you need to rely on procedures or if the job is automatic. If you need to think about how to approach the same task each time, then think about how you can make the task more automatic. You owe it to yourself to make your tasks as intuitive as possible so that thinking about the systems and processes doesn't detract from your ability to use them.

REFLECTION

- How "automatic" are your systems and processes at work?
- Do you waste time thinking about how to layout a document that you've done many times before? What is the hold-up each time?
- How can you improve your systems and processes to enable a more efficient workflow and save time?

Working to Death

A 2021 worldwide study showed North American workers averaged between 33 and 42 hours per week.[30] In this report, workers in India put in over 48 hours per week, and China and some African nations worked between 43 and 47 hours per week.

Interestingly, a business survey in 2012[31] showed that British Columbia's professionals worked long hours, trending at nearly 70-hour workweeks, despite the average statistics being around 37 hours per week. This statistic is surprising and concerning. The people in this group are setting themselves up for serious health and safety problems that likely stem from sleep deprivation. In addition to these concerns, working long hours is counterproductive and does more damage to your organization than you might think.

The more you work, the less efficient you become. The result of overwork is more waste and less productivity. If the cycle continues, the results include absenteeism due to stress and sickness, accidents on the job, and even death. One of the best ways to get yourself off the cycle of overwork is to pay attention to your work when you're at work. Become efficient and productive during your regular working hours, and you'll never again need to put in regular overtime.

Here are ten things you can do right now to improve your productivity by improving your attention to how you spend your time, i.e., do more in less time:

1. Eliminate your physical and electronic clutter. Both are wastes that inhibit your performance. A clean office with sparse décor and no stacks and piles of stuff is more conducive to productivity.

2. Zone in on your work. Organize your work items in zones based on how frequently you access or need an item. For example, if you use a paper cutter only once a month, it is unnecessary to keep it in your office (zone 1).

3. Move email out of your inbox daily. Your inbox should contain ZERO items at the end of your workday. You should handle each email you open immediately. Use the B-F-A-T rule: After you open an email, read it and then (B)ring it forward (if further action is required), (F)ile it (no action is needed), (A)ct on it immediately (if a short response will do), or T(toss)/delete it.

4. Prioritize tomorrow's activities the day before. Then work on your priorities as scheduled. Stick to your schedule.

5. Stop procrastinating at work. Procrastination includes socializing, playing computer games, and personal banter on social media. Unfortunately, these activities only add to your workload. Instead, get help for procrastination—it could be as simple as taking a day off to refresh and recharge.

6. Don't ignore overwhelm. Figure out why you're overwhelmed, resolve your issues, and move forward. For example, if you are constantly behind in your work tasks, maybe you're in the wrong job.

7. Think before you act. Productive people spend a lot of time thinking about and planning how to accomplish tasks before doing them. Planning helps prevent re-doing work.

8. Configure your office space. The most efficient office space is a U-shape. It enables efficient workflow, saving you time.

9. Use project management skills for big projects. For example, if you're new to project task estimating, take a best-guess at how long a task will take and then multiply that time by three to get an accurate timeframe.

10. Use standards and procedures. If your organization does not have standards and procedures for EVERYTHING, you spend more time on tasks than necessary.

Implementing these ten tips will help you decrease your hours at the office, so you have more time to spend with family and friends doing the things you love. And at the end of the day, you owe it to yourself and your employer to return to work mentally refreshed the next day.

REFLECTION

- Is your office well-organized? If not, what can you do to get it there? (A well-organized office improves your time efficiency).
- How do you manage your overwhelm? What is your support system? Can you delegate your work or ask for other types of assistance?
- Do you plan and schedule tomorrow's work the day before? It's the best way to stay on top of things and help reduce overwhelm.
- Is procrastination an issue for you? If so, it may be a sign of overwhelm. Work on both to improve your time.

Brain Dumps – Key to Being Organized

When Michel Eyquem de Montagne (1533-1592) wrote: "Get a purge for your brain. It will do better than for your stomach," he wasn't thinking about modern-day business. However, his words echo true about stressful living, no matter the century. Think about how much "stuff" our brains collect and how that can harm our performance. In that case, who wouldn't benefit from getting a brain purge?

How many times a day, week, or month do you find yourself pulled in several different directions? How often have you written a list to contain your tasks and then equally frequently forgot about or didn't refer to the lists? Unless they are actionable, lists are meaningless. To the rescue: brain dumps.

Brain dumps are like journaling. If you've ever kept a journal, you'll know that it's possibly one of the most powerful ways to accelerate your personal development. By putting your thoughts in writing, you simultaneously free your mind of stress, allowing an opportunity for insights that perhaps you could not (or would not) otherwise be able to see.

A brain dump is like brainstorming, but you brainstorm with yourself instead of with a team. Here's how to do a brain dump: find a pen and paper or use your iPad, laptop, or desktop computer (whatever works for you) and spend up to ten minutes writing everything on your mind. This information dump includes writing all the things you need or want to do and even ideas that may seem ridiculous.

Don't sort your ideas or analyze them as you write; just write them. Once created, this brain dump list becomes your "master" list and a space for "freedom" – a place for gathering action items without the responsibility of actually doing any of them.

Brain dumps allow you to take a bird's eye view of your thoughts, and by doing so, you can make better decisions. When ready, refer to your list and take the appropriate action with each item. Is it a required action? Do you need to do it? Can it be delegated? Can it be deleted from your list?

Review and add to this master list regularly (monthly, weekly – whatever works). Maintaining this list will free you of the constant "to-do's" in your head. In addition, you will be better able to solve problems because you can "see" the issue instead of burying it in your head. You will gain clarity about the items on your list. You will also be able to verify your progress by keeping your list current, i.e., only incomplete items remain on the list.

The best thing about brain dumps and lists is that they help you get "unstuck." They free your mind from the persistent playback mode. And there's nothing better than getting "unstuck" and moving forward.

REFLECTION

- What weighs heavy on your mind most of the time? Have you written/typed it to view? If not, do so to lessen the weight in your brain.
- Take the time to practice a brain dump regularly to help you regain quality time.

Work Smarter, Not Harder

What's the secret to working smarter, not harder? The answer is standardized work methods. If you do not have documented standards for your work, you work much harder than necessary and waste time.

Standards, by their nature, imply something good, and they are precisely good. When we have standards for our work, we have a method that enables us to improve control of our operations. Documented standards provide us with the baseline against which to measure our performance. When we have standards, we can optimize our performance by reducing waste and variability in our operations and improving our product or service quality. As a result, we save time and reduce work stress and overwhelm.

When developing standards for work methods, here are some considerations to help you get started:

1. Follow standards. First, buy-in must come from those using the standards to ensure they will follow them. One way to accomplish this is to engage the impacted individuals in developing standards. This approach enables a "self-governing" process. Also, place a copy of the standards at each workstation (or ensure people know where to find them online).

2. Monitor standards for improvement opportunities. Continuous improvement is key to ensuring that your standards are always current and meet the organization's and customers' needs.

3. Manage exceptions. Manage exceptions by documenting, reviewing, and acting on the exceptions. If exceptions are too frequent, this indicates that the standards need changing.

Without standards, an organization cannot improve. Trying to do so is like trying to hit a moving target. You can improve the current process if it is in control and stable (through standards). It cannot be improved if it is not subject to standards since there is no baseline to gauge improvement.

I cannot overstate the benefits of standardizing work methods through documented procedures to the organization. These benefits include enabling problem-solving, reducing ongoing improvement costs, highlighting waste and problems in processes, making new employee training more straightforward, and improving operator control of operations.

In short, standardization is the best, safest, and easiest way to do your job. It's a way to work smarter, not harder.

REFLECTION

- Does your organization have documented standards for its processes? If not, what could you do to make this a reality for your organization?
- If your organization has standards, when was the last time they were updated?
- Do you feel that documented standards help improve your efficiency at work? Explain.

Efficiency: There is Only One Best Way

It occurs to me that many people revert to habits to repeat inefficient behaviors. Inefficient behaviors require us to use more time and steps to accomplish tasks. Sometimes we don't realize how inefficient we are until someone demonstrates a faster, improved way. Let me explain by retrieving a two-liter milk carton from the refrigerator.

In our house, we store our milk on the inside door of the fridge. Our fridge opens to the right. When I place the milk in the refrigerator, I put it so that the spout is facing the left side of the door when the door is open. Then, when I open the fridge, retrieving the milk carton is simple. Here's how I retrieve the milk carton:

1. Using my right hand, I pick up the carton on its right side, tip it toward me (away from the door), lift it, and pull it up from its position.
2. Holding the carton in my right hand, I use my left hand to open the spout.
3. Using my right hand, I pour the milk.
4. Using my left hand, I close the spout.
5. With the milk still in my right hand, I place the carton in its original position with the spout facing the left side.

As you can see, this is a five-step process using both hands efficiently: pick up, open, pour, close, and replace. But here's what some members of my family do instead.

They place the milk on the refrigerator door with the spout facing to the right, front, or back. Now here's why this is inefficient. When I now use my right hand to pick up the milk container, I have to turn the carton to position the spout to pour. Also, I must use two hands to maneuver the carton into the correct position. The maneuvering takes an extra two turns of the carton.

While this example may seem minuscule and the problem proportionally insignificant, you can see that there is a best or ideal way to place the milk carton for the most efficient retrieval and use by right-handed people in this particular household.

So it is with anything we do at work or home. The next time you reach for that stapler on your desk, consider how many turns of your chair or placements from hand to hand you have to do to retrieve and replace the stapler. Now compound this task with every task you do at work or home, and you'll see how inefficiencies eat at our time, no matter how insignificant the job. It all comes down to habit.

Commit now to changing your inefficient habits. Start with only one task—determine how to make the task more efficient and then practice with the new method for three months before moving on to another task. In the end, you will be more efficient, gain time, and decrease stress. In the words of Pablo Picasso, "*action is the foundational key to all success.*" So, become successful through efficient actions.

REFLECTION

- Of all the daily tasks, what one task takes up most of your time? Why does it take the most time?
- How can you reduce your time on that task?
- Will you commit to reducing your time on the task by practicing new, efficient processes related to the task?
- What other tasks reflect inefficient processes for you? How will you go about improving your efficiency in these tasks?

How "Bottleneck" Executives Can Improve Their Workflow

Have you ever worked for a boss that seemed to be the 'black hole' of the organization? You know the one I'm talking about: documents that go into their office but never seem to come out. If you're that boss, I have good news for you. There is a way to improve your workflow.

In working with executives and others, I found that there are typically three areas where wasted time can impede workflow. These areas include a lack of planning, self-management, and control over the work environment. Let me tell you how to take control of each.

Lack of planning. Planning your workday is key to improving your workflow. However, you need to follow through on your plan to be successful. If you don't plan, you are wasting time and dealing with things during the day as they arise. Therefore, this method is not an effective way to work. Here's how to plan your day instead:

1. Set long-range and short-term goals and objectives. These personal and professional goals should contribute to your and your organization's success.

2. Set daily priorities. These should align with your goals and objectives. Use a priority matrix to help you identify tasks and the tasks' long-range importance and short-range urgency. Prioritization will help you determine a task's overall priorities.

3. Not everything is urgent. Don't treat everything that comes across your desk as urgent. Urgent means "do it now," and it's typically a "life and death" type of situation. Determine if the so-called "urgent" task is important. If the job is not essential, it's not worth doing immediately. Decide when the item is due and schedule it in your calendar for future work.

4. Handling interruptions. Don't allow interruptions to shift your priorities.

5. Choose wisely. If you attempt to do too much, you fail to choose, which becomes a huge timewaster. So again, determine which tasks contribute to your overall goals and do those first.

6. Use realistic time estimates. If you've ever promised to complete a task by a specific time and missed your deadline, guess what? You're not alone. I suggest adding 20–50% to your original time estimate (depending on the complexity of the task) to reflect a more realistic time. This way, you'll never miss another deadline.[32]

Lack of self-management. This area is the main one where many busy executives have difficulty. Here are things you can do to help you better manage your time.

1. Discipline yourself to get work done by setting and sticking to priorities. Use project control charts, mark each completed task, create progress reports, or challenge yourself to stick with deadlines. Reward yourself each time you achieve a milestone – but don't

reward yourself just because you're "close" to reaching the milestone.

2. Get organized in the first place and schedule organizing time into every day. Yes, it's a lot of work. And, yes, it's worth it for success.

3. Clear the clutter from your office. If this area affects you, you need to work with an organizational expert who can help you unclutter your office and set up systems to keep organized. On the other hand, if you don't need an organizational expert to unclutter, why is clutter an issue for you in the first place?

4. Work smarter using the "Only Handle It Once" (OHIO) method to complete your paperwork. We can dispose of 80% of paperwork in the first handling. Yet the average person only disposes 20%. Thus, if you take action the first time you handle a document, you improve your efficiency and productivity and gain more time in your day.

5. Stop procrastinating. Studies show that fear of failure is one big reason for procrastinating. Winston Churchill said he would rather fail in attempting the truly important than succeed at the trivial many times. It's hard to argue with his logic.

6. Delegate. You may find this hard to believe, but you aren't the only one who can do a task well. Trust your subordinates and challenge them to take on more responsibilities if you're an executive. Delegating will free you up to invest your time in more creative work.

Lack of control over the work environment. A lack of control can also impact productivity and create bottlenecks. Here is how to manage your work environment.

1. Control the telephone by scheduling time in your day to receive and return telephone calls. Voice mail is an effective screening tool that helps determine priority calls when you're ready.

2. If visitors drop in, try standing up for the conversation. You'll be pleasantly surprised at how much shorter the visit is when this occurs. Alternatively, tell the visitor that you have to leave within ten minutes or schedule a time to meet the visitor in their office later. If possible, avoid drop-in visits by closing your door.

3. Disorganized meetings result in wasted time. Attend meetings only where needed, but consider delegating attendance to one of your subordinates who can report to you after the meeting. If running the meeting, use proper meeting techniques to stay on track and time.

4. Untrained staff can create inefficiencies. Therefore, ensure that you provide adequate training to all your staff to equip them to handle their roles.

5. Confused responsibility or authority for tasks creates redundancies and wasted time and effort. Ensure that task instructions are clear and indicate who has responsibility and authority.

Now that you know how wasting time may be a factor in being a bottleneck in your organization, list your timewasters and identify the top three. Then, focus on improving those timewasters for about three months before moving to the following three on your list.

Replacing old habits with new habits is difficult but essential. By unlearning old habits, you will improve your time management skills and be a more efficient and productive executive. Treat time as your precious resource, and you'll accomplish more in less time and still have time at the end of the day to do the things you genuinely enjoy.

REFLECTION

- What's your biggest obstacle – lack of planning, self-management, or control over the work environment?
- How can you eliminate that obstacle and regain power over your work?

Overworked

I have worked with many clients over the past few decades, and one common complaint I repeatedly hear is that they are "overworked." Being overworked implies too much work for the role, which is sometimes true, but not usually. What is more usual is that the perception of "overwork" is in the eye of the beholder.

If you feel overworked, the work may not always be the problem. For instance, you may be in a role that is not a good fit for you, or your work methodology may need to change. Unfortunately, in more cases than not, the latter is true. As a result, staff and leaders spend too much time on irrelevant tasks or tasks that others can do, resulting in a backlash of complaints of "overwork" and essential work not getting done.

I recall one client that spent most of his days in meetings. I asked him why he couldn't delegate one or more of his senior staff to meetings on his behalf. He responded that no one else could do it. But here's what I see. His real issue is an inability to delegate, resulting in his working after hours and on weekends to catch up on work he should have done during the day.

In another instance, a client regularly asked for my project status report. His request was despite me emailing the information, like clockwork, on the first of the month. And each time, the email exchange resulted in the client saying that he found it. Overwork? No. This client suffers from poor email management—it was the only area needing improvement.

The next time you claim to be overworked, be honest with yourself.

- How much time are you spending on activities that you could delegate?
- How much time are you spending wading through disorganized email?
- How much time are you spending searching for information to write a report?
- When was the last time you had an authentic meal to power your day?
- What about your fitness routine?
- Do you get enough sleep?

Sure, sometimes we all get a surge of work that requires us to put in a few extra hours, but if this is your norm, you need to shape your approach to your job. You do not need to be disorganized (or overworked).

That said, here is a sobering fact. Nine out of ten change initiatives fail. Thus, framing this in terms of habits, this statistic means you must try at least ten times for each practice you wish to change. However, despite the odds of successfully changing appear stacked against you does not mean you should not try. Persistence is the key to change.

If you're overworked, you can dig yourself out of your difficulty. First, identify the bad habits you need to change, then start by changing one habit. Then when you've changed one habit, practice your new habit for at least three months before moving on to the next one. Over time, you'll be pleasantly surprised that overwork is no longer your norm, even though your responsibilities remain the same.

REFLECTION

- What do you believe is your #1 work responsibility contributing to your feeling of overwork?
- Think about that task and answer the following:
  - Can you delegate it?
  - Can you organize the work better so you're not so overwhelmed?
- If you answered "no" to the above questions, what *can* you do to help relieve your overwork? Will you do it?
- Now answer the same questions for your #2 work responsibility, etc.
- Remember, if you cannot make the required change(s), reach out to an organizational expert or counselor to help you gain a new sense of work balance.

Taming the Workaholic

Hi. My name is Mary, and I *used to be* a workaholic.

Ever since I can remember, I would spend endless hours "doing." First, it was school projects, then work projects for my employer, and then in the 1980s, when I started my own business, I spent endless hours working in, on, and for my business. And somewhere in between, I also spent countless hours volunteering for various associations and attending classes to complete my university degrees and other certifications—this on top of my already full work and family schedules.

So why am I telling you this? Because along the way, I learned from experience and research that being a workaholic is not only counterproductive but can ultimately kill you or, at the very least, make you very tired and maybe even very sick. Here's what else I learned.

Working more than 35 to 40 hours a week does not contribute proportionally to productivity. For example, studies have shown that industrial workers who worked eight-hour days produced the same number of widgets as those who worked 10-hour days. However, occasional overtime can yield results, but the gains won't be directly proportional to the time worked. For example, if your workweek extends 50% from 40 to 60 hours, then productivity would only be a 25–30% increase. This slight productivity increase is because people typically do their best work between hours two and six of an eight-hour workday. After that, fatigue may affect productivity. In addition, sustaining overtime over a long time results in less productivity because of sustained mental exhaustion.

It turns out that factory workers may be able to turn out a reasonably productive eight-hour day. In contrast, knowledge workers are not as effective—their productivity maxes out at about six hours a day.

On top of this, research by the U.S. military has shown that cognitive decline is equivalent to a .10 blood alcohol level with even just one hour less sleep per night. This finding means that if you're not getting enough sleep, whether a factory or knowledge worker, you may be making the same quality decisions as an intoxicated person. So think about that the next time you show up for a full day's work when you didn't get quality sleep the night before.

Workaholics, be aware—you are doing yourself and your organization a disservice. You will be far more productive sticking to a 35-to-40-hour work week. If you're having difficulty adjusting *down*, speak to a coach or therapist and get back to getting your life back. You'll be glad you did.

REFLECTION

- Do you get enough sleep – i.e., 7.5–8 hours each night?
- Do you find you more productive at certain times of the day? Take note of those times and schedule your important work for that time.
- Are you fuelling your body appropriately? It's hard to work any time when one skips meals or relies on snacks all day for energy.
- Are you taking breaks during the day? Ultimately, look away from your work every 20 minutes (even for a minute) and do something else (e.g., look out the window, check your email or phone messages) just to recharge your brain.

Remove Complexity to Save Time

There are many roads to saving time, but eliminating complexity from personal and business processes is the best way to improve personal efficiency. And the way to eliminate complexity is to identify areas in your personal and/or business processes that cost the most and/or create the most customer dissatisfaction in the shortest time. Let me give you an example of a business process that impacts personal processes.

I recently worked with a client to assist him with developing better personal practices to enable him to be more efficient with his work. The biggest problem he was experiencing was not getting his work done on time. His employer felt that he was taking too long to produce the finished product, resulting in a high cost to the organization.

Also, his customers (bosses and co-workers) were becoming increasingly dissatisfied with his performance because he took too long to finish tasks. It would be easy to say that my client should use better time management skills and focus on performing these important tasks, and the problem would be solved. But it's not so clear-cut.

Upon analysis, I discovered that my client was using good time management skills and working diligently on essential tasks, but the tasks themselves were suspect. In one instance, the task required several repetitive steps, including review and feedback from others. This back-and-forth prevented my client from completing what otherwise could have been a simple task.

One particular task involved a simple spreadsheet that others implemented years ago, and it steadily grew in complexity with new rules and new decision-makers added along the way. You guessed it. Each time the organization added new rules and decision points, complexity increased, and the amount of work also increased. This spreadsheet undermined my client's productivity while increasing the costs of delivering the completed task. Instead of adding new and more rules to an existing process, the entire process should have been re-evaluated and simplified. This "re-do" would have saved time, money, and customer (and client) angst.

You can see from this example that helping clients become more productive is not necessarily about the clients' work habits but the organizational systems and processes that have become complex over time. To remedy the situation, I suggest conducting a diagnosis to identify the causes of the symptoms (i.e., the "problems"). Then develop an action plan and implement the action items to remove complexity.

In any organization, a modest estimate is that 40–60% of activities and costs associated with services and processes do not add value to the services or processes and do very little to satisfy the customer. By eliminating complexity, an organization can realize significant productivity improvements in just a few short months, saving everyone time and money.

REFLECTION

- Do you sometimes (or regularly) work on a task that takes way more time than it should? Why do you think the task takes too long?
- When you work on tasks, do you do them as rote jobs, or do you consider the value you add to the customer?
- Do you know your customer(s) for each task?
- What value do you add to the task that is valuable for the customer?
- How can you improve your time efficiency in your routine tasks?

Kill the Waste Quadrant to Improve Efficiency

The time management matrix isn't new. Stephen Covey introduced it in the 1980s. But despite many people understanding time management principles, they still have difficulty implementing these skills. I believe implementation is challenging because people become overwhelmed by their important and urgent tasks, so they resort to tasks of least resistance—those that are not important and not urgent—the "waste" tasks.

Let's have a look at the time management matrix to understand the "waste" quadrant better:

Let's face it: if you're spending too much time in

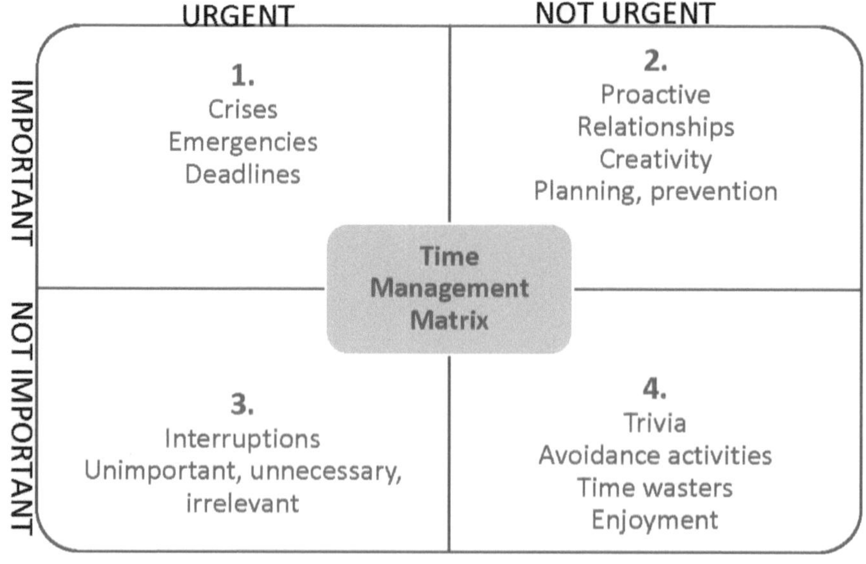

Quadrant 4 (the "waste" quadrant), you can eat up a lot of your time and create a backlog at work, leading to stress and overwhelm. The best way to stop wasting time on tasks that are neither important nor urgent is to spend ten minutes daily planning your activities for the next day. *Ten minutes*. That's all it takes.

Spend most of your days working on activities that lead to accomplishing your goals. You do this by focusing on Quadrant 2 tasks (important but not urgent). Sure, you'll say that's easier said than done. However, it is easy to accomplish if you prepare. Here's how a day working in Quadrant 2 might look.

- Upon rising in the morning, exercise
- Shower/hygiene
- Breakfast
- Work – tackle the first things on your plan and work through your priority items (remember that you spent 10 minutes yesterday planning your work today)
- Lunch – take lunch with colleagues or friends (skipping lunch to date your computer is non-productive and can lead to a stressful and overwhelming afternoon)
- After lunch – continue with your work plan
- End of the day – spend 10 minutes on your plan for the next day
- Go home, spend time with your family, and do things that you enjoy
- Go to sleep at the same time each night so you are refreshed and energized to tackle tomorrow (remember to get at least 7.5–8 hours of sleep every night)
- Repeat

If you can practice this routine for three months, you'll have built a habit that will help you accomplish your goals, live a relatively stress-free life, and be happier. Now that's something not to waste.

REFLECTION

- In which time management quadrant do you work most – 1, 2, 3, or 4?
- If you spend more time in any quadrant other than 2, you may need to evaluate how you work.
- Remember to plan your workdays, schedule your work, and then stick to your schedule.
- How can you improve your workdays to spend more time in Quadrant 2?

Help! I'm a Procrastinator!

Procrastination is about putting off (or deferring) something to a later time. We all do it occasionally: procrastination is normal. However, if procrastination starts interfering with your life and work more frequently, you need to address it immediately.

There are many reasons people procrastinate, but here are six of the top reasons that I have discovered that could impact your work productivity.

1. Perfectionism. I confess that I sometimes focus on getting things done perfectly, so much so that it takes me much longer to complete something (and makes me tired as a result!). However, this may be a more serious problem when perfectionism causes one not to start work on tasks/projects because of a perceived need to wait to get something exactly right. "If it's not right, then I'm not going to do it" can cause project paralysis.

2. Anticipating the worst. Another reason why people procrastinate is that they anticipate the worst. They imagine disaster as an outcome of their performance, so they don't proceed with it. This anticipation can also be related to perfectionism.

3. Overwhelm or underwhelm. Let's face it. Sometimes tasks or projects can be too much or too little. Procrastination can occur if one perceives tasks and projects as overwhelming or underwhelming. For example, if you're working on a large project and have no idea

how to get started or see the project as one massive "to-do," you may be afraid to start the work for fear of failure. Likewise, if the project or task is so mind-numbingly dull, you may be tempted to put it off in favour of doing more exciting work.

4. Immediate gratification. Some people may need to see immediate results from their work. If this isn't possible, then they procrastinate on starting. This approach is particularly true for procrastinators working on projects with long timelines. If the project results won't provide immediate satisfaction with a completed job, the tendency is to delay starting the task.

5. Passivity. Sometimes an individual may have difficulty starting a task until they get a push from someone else (especially if the task is too big or too small and, therefore, overwhelming or underwhelming). This approach is called passivity.

6. Hostility. Perhaps one of the worst reasons for procrastination is hostility. People angry at the world for their lot in life may decide they just won't do anything. This anger is the worst reason for procrastination and may require therapeutic intervention if it's a habit.

If you're a procrastinator, here are three ways to combat procrastination and get back on the road to productivity:

1. Use project management principles on all tasks (large or small).
2. Stop worrying about what might happen.
3. Just do it.

Here is a simple guideline on how to use project management principles on all tasks:

1. Determine your deadline, if there is one.

2. Determine the steps to complete the project by breaking it down into parts. For example, if the task involves interviewing, writing reports, and reviewing information with stakeholders, then write all those tasks in the order they need to be done.

3. Determine how long each part of the project will take. In our example, determine how long it will take to conduct interviews, write reports, and review information with stakeholders. If it takes you five days to conduct interviews, ten days to write reports, and 15 days to review reports with stakeholders, you will need 30 days to complete the project. However, remember to add a "cushion" of time to your original estimate to account for unanticipated events. A rule of thumb is multiplying your initial time estimate by three to get a more realistic timeline.

4. In our example, count 30 days backward from your deadline based on your estimated required time to complete the project. This time will be your absolute "must" start date to ensure your project's completion.

5. Get started as scheduled on your starting date. If you can start sooner, that will be even better because it will provide a 'cushion' for unexpected occurrences.

6. Stick to your schedule. No matter what.

Now that you've scheduled your project and task(s), the best thing to do is start. Starting something helps initiate momentum; the more you work on a task, the more momentum you build, making it easier to stick to the task. If perfection creeps in and makes you worry about the outcome, help yourself stop worrying by challenging your thoughts to find the evidence for your perceived outcome. Ask yourself: "What would I say to a friend who had this worry?" You'll be pleasantly surprised at how quickly the worry will disappear.

Finally, just get on with it and do it. There's no better way to overcome procrastination than by getting into action. Action is the enemy of procrastination. Make action your friend.

If you follow these three easy steps to overcoming procrastination, you will be more productive, efficient, creative, energized at work and home, and have more time in your life.

REFLECTION

- Is there a pattern to your procrastination? Are there specific tasks that just scream "wait" at you? Describe those tasks. What is it about these tasks that make you defer working on them?
- Have you tried scheduling work to help you beat procrastination?
- Identify your "top 3" reasons for procrastinating on work. How will you reduce (or eliminate) your procrastination to become more productive and use your time better?

Moving to Efficiency

Why are some people "uber" efficient and productive while others sloth through their days? It occurs to me that since none of us is born lazy or efficient, we can unlearn certain behaviors.

If you're efficient, kudos to you. Keep up the great work. But if you're a procrastinator, please read on so I can share with you some ways you can become uber-efficient in your place of work and improve your life dramatically. However, first, let me tell you why you may choose not to embrace efficiency in the first place.

First, change is hard, no matter how small or big. It's also uncomfortable. Sometimes we don't change because it never occurs to us that we need to change. If you've cruised through work and life thus far and lightning hasn't struck, you may have convinced yourself that things are good.

However, suppose you've convinced yourself that becoming more efficient may help catapult your career beyond the boardroom. In that case, you realize that you will need to take time away from things that do not contribute to your career, like worrying about how many likes you got on social media. Thus, this is the second reason you resist change. It seems like such an inconvenience, a chore, to disconnect from social media, and the payoff for becoming efficient just doesn't seem worth the effort.

The third reason you might be resisting changing your behavior is fear of failure or rejection. What if you change and you don't implement efficiency techniques effectively? Won't you look silly? Well, listen. The only people who will look silly are those who are not implementing efficiency in their work and life. They will remain in their jobs (or be at a threat of demotion over time). But not you. You will be moving forward to a better future.

A fourth reason for resisting change is that it takes a lot of work to be efficient. And most people don't want to work that hard, especially if you're starting from the point of procrastination. That's a complete 180-degree turnaround!

If you're serious about becoming more efficient, but don't know where to start, here are three things to consider:

1. Find someone to show, teach, coach, or mentor you to be more efficient. Or do research in the library or on the Internet. Learn how to be more efficient.

2. Identify someone who is already efficient. Ask them to share their efficiency techniques with you. It could be a colleague at work or someone you admire.

3. If you know an efficient colleague, ask them if you can watch them work for a day to see how they manage their workload. Most leaders are happy to teach their techniques to their peers. Learn their secrets to being more efficient.

Once the principles are down, start practicing by getting out of your comfort zone. Remember that it takes about three months to develop a good habit. Stick with it. You are worth the investment.

REFLECTION

- What is holding you back from being efficient?
- Do you have someone you can rely on to help you become more efficient?
- To help you become more efficient, pick one small bad habit you currently have and work on changing that habit for three months. For example, if you forget to pick up your clothes off your bedroom floor, try picking up and hanging your clothes every day for three months. Then move on to improving another habit. Remember: "baby steps" will get you there. Best of luck to you!

The Mindfulness Shift

Have you noticed that time seems to go faster as you get older? I had a theory about this decades ago as I pondered the "why" of this phenomenon. I determined that as we age, we accumulate more experiences and memories. Then as we play back these experiences and memories—drawing on them to comprehend the present—we usurp time in playback. Thus we experience time as going faster, but as we know, time doesn't go faster; it just sometimes feels like it speeds up.

Curiously, scientists have identified many reasons for our time perception accelerating as we reach middle age. They believe that as we get older, we "chunk" our experiences into broad categories and then further gather them into even larger generic groups in our minds. I equate this to a function-based hierarchical filing system, similar to library systems.

For example, imagine a four-year-old playing on a swing set in a park with his grandfather watching. The four-year-old would likely focus on the minutiae of the experience – the back-and-forth of the swing, the wind in his hair and nostrils, the birds in the sky, the fluffy clouds, the sand under the swing, and so on. But on the other hand, the grandfather would focus on the entire swing set and its surroundings, equating it to another playground in a park. In other words, the four-year-old focuses on details, whereas the grandfather focuses on the bigger picture (the large generic group of a broad category).

A study in 2018[33] argued that as we age, we chunk our experiences into such categories as work, family, and fun outings. Consequently, it feels as if fewer things happened to us in that time. Moreover, this chunking increases nostalgia as we get older—the accelerated time seems to instigate an urge to reflect on our momentous occasions, our "self across time."

Another study published in the United Kingdom in July 2020[34] investigated the sense of time passage during the COVID-19 lockdowns. The researchers found that older people and those for whom social isolation was especially hard found time dragging, reflecting boredom. This time drag contrasts with previous findings that time speeds up as we age. The researcher explained that because lockdowns curtailed socializing and normal daily activities, especially for the elderly, the loss of freedom and inability to engage with technology left them more vulnerable to experiencing slow passing of time.

In addition, the study found that younger people, those more satisfied with their social interactions, and those with less stress experienced time passing more quickly. However, if we ask these people a year or two later about their experience with the passing time over the previous year or two, their retrospective judgments would be influenced by the amount of memory content from that time. Thus, this would support the initial theory that we would have fewer memories with less happening in a given period, and the period might feel short. These findings demonstrate that substantial changes to daily life significantly impact our experience of time, with younger, more socially satisfied people more likely to experience time passing more quickly during the lockdown.

This study brings us full circle—as we get older, why do we ask where the last 10, 20, or more years went? This retrospective judgment of passing time can profoundly influence how we evaluate our lives. For example, in Landau's 2018 study (see note 30), the scientists suggested that chunking our experiences makes us feel like we had fewer of them. We " chunk " because fewer experiences feel new (e.g., a day at the park).

However, what if we really focus on our experiences, i.e., become mindful?

If we focus on the moment—the experience—we can apprehend its uniqueness and delight like the four-year-old rather than observe like the grandfather. We attune to the moment rather than the chunk. According to Amishi Jha,[35] we can understand the relationship between mindful attention and long-term memory storage as follows:

Better perception → Better encoding → Better working memory → Better long-term memory → Fuller embodied retrieval

Therefore, when we get into the habit of paying attention to our experiences nonjudgmentally, we improve our working memory, helping us store and recall long-term memories of events and information.

Being mindful can help "re-sensitize" us to appreciate even the simple things like watching our four-year-old play on the swing set in the park and counteract our perception of life's quickening pace. In addition, if we allow ourselves to be fully in the moment, we might be able to appreciate the uniqueness of the moment when it passes.

REFLECTION

- What did you do today?
- What did you do yesterday?
- Did you chunk your activities?
- How could you have experienced your activities more uniquely today? Yesterday?
- The Mayo Clinic[36] suggests the following steps to practice mindfulness:
  - Pay attention. It's hard to slow down and notice things in a busy world. Try to take the time to experience your environment with all of your senses—touch, sound, sight, smell, and taste. For example, when you eat a favorite food, take the time to smell, taste, and truly enjoy it.
  - Live in the moment. Try to intentionally bring an open, accepting, and discerning attention to everything you do. Find joy in simple pleasures.
  - Accept yourself. Treat yourself the way you would treat a good friend.
  - Focus on your breathing. When you have negative thoughts, try to sit down, take a deep breath and close your eyes. Focus on your breath as it moves in and out of your body. Sitting and breathing for even just a minute can help.

- You can also try more structured mindfulness exercises, such as:
  - Body scan meditation. Lie on your back with your legs extended and arms at your sides, palms facing up. Focus your attention slowly and deliberately on each part of your body, from toe to head or head to toe. Be aware of any sensations, emotions, or thoughts associated with each part of your body.
  - Sitting meditation. Sit comfortably with your back straight, feet flat on the floor, and hands in your lap. Breathing through your nose, focus on your breath moving in and out of your body. If physical sensations or thoughts interrupt your meditation, note the experience and then return your focus to your breath.
  - Walking meditation. Find a quiet place 10 to 20 feet in length, and begin to walk slowly. Focus on the experience of walking, being aware of the sensations of standing, and the subtle movements that keep your balance. When you reach the end of your path, turn and continue walking, maintaining awareness of your sensations.

The Time of Our Lives: Pandemic Flashback

The COVID-19 pandemic response heightened our awareness of time. In short, we learned that time is subjective in many ways. For instance, if you're the type who enjoys working from home, your days likely felt as if they flew by. On the other hand, those that craved travel and visiting friends probably felt as if time stood still.

Neuroscientists confirm that no matter if our sense of time feels like time is flying by or standing still, no single organ in our bodies can keep time. However, our working memory plays a significant role in perceiving time. For instance, if someone asks us to estimate the duration of an event, we would tap into our working memory to make a retrospective judgment for short durations.

However, researchers found that individuals using this type of temporal judgment rely on remembered non-temporal information rather than material information encoded in memory. Our perceptions of time depend on the amount of information, the number of contextual changes, or the memory load.[37]

Think back to when you stayed home as directed by governments to stop the spread of the coronavirus. Now compare your time at home to when you returned to work. Which time went more quickly? You would likely say that your time at home went by very slowly compared to your time at work. This belief relies on a comparison recalled from your long-term memory. You might even compare this to watching the ticks on a clock and say there were more ticks on the clock while you were home than at work, even though we know the number of ticks was the same.

Another time phenomenon is the oddball effect. This phenomenon explains how we deal with repetition. In brief, we perceive novel or unexpected stimuli as having longer time durations. Once again, think back to when you were at home. Then think about returning to work or other routine activities. For example, the new activity, returning to work, makes us focus on creating a new memory and feel like time slows down. Therefore, the recent memory makes us feel like staying home has passed quickly. In other words, we suppress the memory of staying home because we now have a new activity; hence, we feel that the time we stayed home just flew by.

In addition to retrospective judgment and the oddball effect, our attention and emotions affect our sense of time. For instance, anything that grabs our attention or requires us to pay attention will feel much longer. The pandemic measures certainly did that. Regarding emotions, time will fly by if you are happy or having a good time, but it will feel like it's standing still if you are lonely or sad. However, some people in 2020–2021 may have experienced time standing still despite having busy days. For example, frontline workers may have operated in fear and heightened attentiveness. This awareness would have served to slow their perception of time passing.

As we age, our memory also distorts our perception of time, affecting our sense of when an event occurred. Psychologists indicate that when we recall an event in the distant past, it feels like it happened more recently. However, events that occurred within the past three years feel more remote. Psychologists refer to this effect as telescoping. The effect occurs whenever we make temporal assumptions about past events.

A theory behind the telescoping effect is the accessibility principle—time perceptions regarding certain events depend on the event's information accessibility.[38] For example, 9/11 is a salient memory for many people. I still remember what I was doing and how I felt when the first plane hit. Remembering my feelings about the event makes it feel like it happened fairly recently (forward telescoping). On the other hand, if you had a busy and eventful weekend, you may not remember last Friday (backward telescoping) on Monday. This memory inaccessibility is because of the things that happened on the weekend, blurring your recollection of Friday.

To put this into the pandemic perspective, can you recall when you last purchased toilet paper, given the shortage early in the pandemic? Due to time perception, you probably cannot remember (unless it was yesterday or today!). In addition, the event is no longer accessible—many more significant events have likely transpired in your life since your last purchase of toilet paper.

As we look back on the pandemic and its management, remember that the illusion of time will impact your recollection of events. So perhaps our misplacement of pandemic events in memory is not such a bad thing.

About the Author

Mary Čolak is the author of several newsletters and blogs on business, contentious issues, and life. *Beyond Success: Acquiring Time* is her second book in the *Beyond Success* series. Her first book is *Considerations in Making Money.*

For over 30 years, Mary used her unique ability to turn chaos into order for organizations and individuals. She helps clients identify necessary organizational and personal work methods and systems improvements. As a result of her involvement, clients experience marked improvements in efficiency, productivity, and a reduction in their stress. In addition to working with organizations to improve business processes, Mary coaches individuals to help them manage and overcome obstacles in their job performance. In addition, Mary taught operations management for seven years as a university instructor in the Bachelor of Business Administration program.

Mary is a lifelong learner. She has a Master of Arts degree in professional communication, a Bachelor of Arts degree in psychology (major) and English (minor), and an Associate of Arts diploma in public administration. In addition, she has a master's certificate in Lean Six Sigma and was certified as a management consultant in 2004. Her awards and recognitions include the Outstanding Graduate award from the Institute of Public Administrators of Canada and an honour roll certificate from the Canadian Association of Management Consultants for placing first in British Columbia on the comprehensive national management consulting case study examination.

Mary was born in Croatia and emigrated to Canada with her parents at a very young age. Today, she loves spending summers in her native Croatia but is happy to call Canada her home, where she lives and enjoys her life with her husband, children, and grandchildren.

Endnotes

---

[1] This device, invented by Egyptian scribes and priests around 1500 BC, was called a clepsydra. It used the steady dripping of water from a vessel to drive a mechanical device that indicates the hour. The water clock remained in use until the development of mechanical clocks nearly 3,000 years later.

[2] Atomic clocks have enabled new, highly accurate measuring time and distance techniques. These techniques, involving radar, lasers, spacecraft, radio telescopes, and pulsars, have been applied to studying problems in celestial mechanics, astrophysics, relativity, and cosmogony.

[3] The meridian at this longitude (0°) is the prime meridian or Greenwich meridian. In 1928 the International Astronomical Union changed the designation of the standard time of the Greenwich meridian to Universal Time, which remains in general use in a modified form as Coordinated Universal Time (UTC), accommodating the timekeeping differences that arise between atomic time (derived from atomic clocks) and solar time.

[4] Timmons, G. (2019, 2014). *Hammurabi biography.* Biography. https://www.biography.com/political-figure/hammurabi

[5] The Hebrew Bible is the first to use the word "shekel" in the Book of Genesis. The term "shekel" refers to a unit of weight, around 9.6 or 9.8 grams (0.34 or 0.35 oz), used in Bronze Age Europe for balance weights and fragments of bronze that may have served as money. It is also a monetary unit of Israel, sheqel (also spelled shekel). The monetary unit contains 100 agorot. Israel replaced the old sheqel with the New Israeli Sheqel (NIS) in 1985.

[6] See my book, *Beyond Success: Considerations in Making Money*, which talks more about the history of money.

[7] Early clay tablets came from the site of Uruk in southern Iraq. When no longer valid (or fully completed) for writing, the tablets were repurposed as packing material for the foundations of new buildings.

[8] Cuneiform is a logo-syllabic script used to write several languages of the Ancient North East. The script was in active use from the early Bronze Age until the beginning of the Common Era. Its name derives from its characteristic wedge-shaped impression (Latin: cuneus), which forms its signs.

[9] "Time is money" is an aphorism originated by Benjamin Franklin in an essay (Advice to a Young Tradesman) that appeared in George Fisher's 1748 book, "The American Instructor: or Young Man's Best Companion," in which Franklin wrote, "remember that time is money." However, there are claims that the phrase was already in print in 1719 in the Whig newspaper "The Free-Thinker," writing "In vain did his Wife inculcate to him, That Time is Money" (The Free-Thinker, vol. III, from Lady-day to Michaelmas, 1719. London. 1723. p. 128). The saying is intended to convey the monetary cost of laziness, by pointing out that when one is paid for the amount of time one spends working, minimizing non-working time also minimizes the amount of money that is lost to other pursuits (source: Wikipedia).

[10] See Taylor's book: The Principles of Scientific Management that he wrote in 1911.

[11] Macan, T. H. (1994). Time management: Test of a process model. *Journal of Applied Psychology, 79*(3), 381–391. https://doi.org/10.1037/0021-9010.79.3.381

[12] Buddy clock-in system or buddy punching is when a coworker punches your timecard (aka clocks in) in your absence.

[13] Bloom, N. (updated article 2021, March 21). Our research shows working from home works in moderation. *The Guardian.*

[14] For more information, see Pew Research statistics at: https://www.pewresearch.org/social-trends/2020/12/09/how-the-coronavirus-outbreak-has-and-hasnt-changed-the-way-americans-work/

[15] Updated info, 2017; source: Kelly, J. F. (2017, June 14). Addiction in the workplace: What you need to know. *Psychology Today.*

[16] Refer to Centers for Disease Control and Prevention – Marijuana and public health.

[17] Zuckermann, A. M. E., Battista, K. V., Belanger, R. E., Haddad, S., Butler, A., Costello, M. J., & Leatherdale, S. T. (2021). Trends in youth cannabis use across cannabis legalization: Data from the COMPASS prospective cohort study. *Preventive Medicine Reports, 22,* 101351.)

[18] For more information on cannabis use in Canada, refer to the Canada Cannabis Survey 2020: https://www.canada.ca/en/health-canada/services/drugs-medication/cannabis/research-data/canadian-cannabis-survey-2020-summary.html.

[19] Steinhorst, C. (2020, February 20). *How multitasking erodes productivity and dings your IQ.* Forbes, Inc.

[20] Winch, G. (2014). *Emotional first aid: Practical strategies for treating failure, rejection, guilt, and other everyday psychological injuries.* Plume.

[21] Hamilton, J. (2010). *Multitasking brain divides and conquers to a point.* www.npr.org

[22] O'Brien, J. (2011, April). *UCSF study on multitasking reveals switching glitch in the aging brain.* University of California San Francisco.

[23] Wood, S. (2013, January 23). *Frequent multitaskers are bad at it.* University of Utah.

[24] Covey, S. (2011, January 25). The 90-10 principle. [Video]. *YouTube.* https://www.youtube.com/watch?v=iKvEYKoiJ48

[25] Adapted from Mackenzie, A., & Mackenzie M. (1995). *Investing time for maximum return.* Coastal Training Technologies Corp.

[26] Headline adapted from *CNN Money,* October 28, 2002: The last taboo – It's not sex, it's not drinking, it's stress – and it's soaring. https://money.cnn.com/magazines/fortune/fortune_archive/2002/10/28/330967/index.htm

[27] A 2012 survey by the office space provider Regus found that 75% of Chinese workers said their stress level had increased over the past year, compared with a global average of 48%.

[28] For more information, refer to https://www.apa.org/pubs/reports/work-well-being/compounding-pressure-2021

[29] For more information, check out the Radicati Group and financesonline.com.

[30] Anttila, T., Harma, M., & Oinas, T. (2021). Working hours – tracking the current and future trends. *Industrial Health, 59*(5), 285–292.

[31] BC Business Magazine, 2012.

[32] In project management, it is not unusual to take your original estimate and multiply it by three to achieve a more realistic timeline.

[33] Landau, M. J., Arndt, J., Swanson, T. J., & Bultmann, M. N. (2018) Why life speeds up: Chunking and

the passage of autobiographical time, *Self and Identity, 17*(3), 294–309, DOI: 10.1080/15298868.2017.1308878

[34] Ogden, R. S. (2020, July 6). The passage of time during the UK Covid-19 lockdown. *PLOS*. DOI: 10.1371/journal.pone.0235871.

[35] Jha, A. (2021, October 25). Find your focus: Own your attention in 12 minutes a day. *Mindful.org.*

[36] Mayo Clinic. *Mindfulness exercises.* https://www.mayoclinic.org/healthy-lifestyle/consumer-health/in-depth/mindfulness-exercises/art-20046356

[37] Miller, G. W., Hicks, R. E., & Willette, M. (1978). Effects of concurrent verbal rehearsal and temporal set upon judgments of temporal duration. *Acta Psychologica, 42,* 173–179.

[38] Brown, N. R., Rips, L. J., & Shevell, S. K. (1985). The subjective dates of natural events in very-long-term memory. *Cognitive Psychology, 17*(2), 139-177.

www.ingramcontent.com/pod-product-compliance
Ingram Content Group UK Ltd.
Pitfield, Milton Keynes, MK11 3LW, UK
UKHW042017190726
13854UKWH00005B/2322